PRAISE FOR
LET'S ~~KILL~~ KISS ALL THE LAWYERS

Conventional advice to lawyers who want to be loved is "get a dog, their love is unconditional". In this book, Virginia Warren has taken on the huge task of making lawyers loved by people! In a fun, rollicking work Virginia tracks her path as a lawyer from 'Ice Queen' to 'Human Being'. In the process she gives advice on how any lawyer can achieve this. In the movie City Slickers, *Curly said, "the meaning of life is one thing, and that's what you have to find". Every lawyer should read this book because it contains that 'one thing' that a lawyer needs to find to be 'loved'. Happy reading, and lawyer, heal thy self and be loved.*

– Tom Gyorffy QC, Melbourne, Australia

Virginia's humour is infectious and life-giving. She has opened the door to a prickly topic with finesse and light-hearted comic relief which we all need as lawyers. Her vulnerability revealed in these pages is courageous.

– Dr Victoria Lambropoulos, barrister and senior lecturer, Australian National University

Anyone who meets Virginia will quickly become aware of her enthusiasm, passion and ability to 'think outside the square'.

Virginia helps us understand that, regarding relational and interpersonal conflicts (as well as in life in general!), dealing with the surface disturbances alone will only go so far. She indicates that delving deep to reveal and address what underlies the superficial problems will get to the core of the issues and then enable positive change. Virginia has the skill of helping people get to the heart of their issues in her light-hearted manner. Humour really does help the medicine go down.

We are moving from a time of competition and adversarial agendas to a time of collaboration and integration – with the aim of 'win-win' outcomes. We have a strong tendency to adhere to the status quo and it takes considerable courage to question and change entrenched systems that might be long overdue for an upgrade. And as for courage, Virginia has it in spades. This, combined with her passion and vision, will bring about the change that society is calling for.

Not only lawyers but also all professionals would benefit from this work. As in health care, a holistic, integrative and collaborative approach has the potential to bring about sustained and effective change from which many will benefit. Virginia helps us to understand that the time has come.

– Dr Catherine J Fyans, integrative medical practitioner and author of *The Wounding of Health Care:* From Fragmentation to Integration

Humor mixed with wisdom ... or is it wisdom mixed with humor? Either way, this book provides much needed smiles and advice.

– J. Kim Wright, American Bar Association author, leader in the integrative law movement. www.jkimwright.com

Having ditched my own 'Armani Armour' when I moved from corporate legal counsel with a major listed company to general practitioner in regional Victoria some five years ago now, I get this! Along with (slightly) more sensible shoes came a realisation that we're seen in less than an appealing light by the community despite the fact that many of us man our local free legal clinics, spend lots of hours doing pro-bono work and volunteer on local boards and sporting committees. And to those clients who do pay us, we have to spell out (in writing, of course), how to sue us if we fall short of their often excessive expectations. How do we grow if we are afraid of making mistakes! It's depressing and soul destroying. No other business has such a model.

Virginia puts this bitter pill into perspective. She does so in a courageous yet light-hearted way, and her work gives us hope along with a renewed respect for our profession and our work in serving others. Many of our colleagues do actually feel the same way, and alone by the photocopier at 8.00 pm with five more copies of that court bible still to churn out we thought it was just 'me'. Funny and entertaining, Virginia is nevertheless well read on her subject and I was gratified and relieved to see references to Jung, the HearthMath Institute and Dr Joe Dispenza – who would have thought that other lawyers read this stuff too!

Virginia encourages us to come out of our fluorescent-lit offices into the real light, and see a new way forward working from the heart.

– Deborah Culhane, lawyer, Duly Served Legal and Consulting

I love what Virginia is doing in her work to address the discontent of many lawyers by helping them to get back in touch with their true selves. As lawyers, the more connected we are to ourselves and to our source, the greater the capacity for us to help our clients and provide transformative outcomes. Virginia delivers a powerful message in a fun and witty way, which is captivating. If anyone can help lawyers with their 'emotional empowerment' it is Virginia. This is important work and I commend Virginia for having the courage to step into the arena.

– Alicia Dumais Temmerman, lawyer and spirit medium

This is the book I have been waiting to read. As a lawyer, yoga teacher and practitioner, I am always on the lookout for others who understand the healing potential of legal work. Virginia gets it. Through her laugh-out-loud style, she bravely shows us the potential for transformation in ourselves, our clients and the hardships that often bring us together. This book offers a different perspective on work we do as lawyers and, as Virginia puts it, "the alchemy of conflict". If you're looking for a deeper perspective of what it means to be a lawyer or are seeking peace in your personal and professional life, this book is an invaluable resource.

– Carrie L. DeJesus, Esquire, holistic law practitioner and yoga teacher

Virginia Warren is a shining light from Australia: lawyer, yoga instructor, shadow enlightener, spiritual light bearer and great friend—all dusted with her Gemini sense of humor. Watch out: she's present!!

– Stuart Webb, founder of Collaborative Law

Reading Virginia's book is like walking through an enchanted forest –
every corner you turn, you discover the beauty of insight and wisdom. She
weaves ancient philosophies together with contemporary scientific research
to create a wonderful guideline for how we can be better at self-care, self-
connect and self-transformation. As a lawyer myself, I salute Virginia
for her courage to write a book for her fellow lawyers on love, feelings,
shadow-self and other essential matters that are rarely written about for
intellectually-minded lawyers. In truth, the highest form of intelligence is
represented by a fine balance between the left brain and right brain, an
alchemical synthesis of intellect and intuition, and a synchronised dance
between the dark and the light. I believe Virginia is offering a way to reach
this intelligence, not through external counsels, but from deep within, a
change from inside out. Thank you, Virginia.

– Elva Zhang, lawyer, founder of Peace Lab

Published in Australia by
Zen Publishing
10 Blamey Place, Mornington, 3931, VIC, Australia.
letschat@virginia-warren.com
www.virginia-warren.com

First published in Australia 2019

National Library of Australia Cataloguing in Publication entry

 A catalogue record for this book is available from the National Library of Australia

ISBN: 978-0-6483962-0-8 (paperback)
ISBN: 978-0-6483962-1-5 (hardback)
ISBN: 978-0-6483962-2-2 (epub)

Cover layout and design by Sophie White
Printed by IngramSpark

kiss
"LET'S ~~KILL~~
ALL THE
LAWYERS!"

...*said no-one, ever.*

A story of unrequited love

VIRGINIA WARREN

The Zen Lawyer

"Advice? I don't have advice.
Stop aspiring and start writing.
If you're writing, you're a writer.

Write like you're a goddamn death row inmate
and the governor is out of the country
and there's no chance for a pardon.

Write like you're clinging to the edge of a cliff,
white knuckles, on your last breath,
and you've got just one last thing to say,
like you're a bird flying over us and you can see everything,
and please, for God's sake,
tell us something that will save us from ourselves.

Take a deep breath and tell us your deepest,
darkest secret, so we can wipe our brow and know that we're not alone.

Write like you have a message from the king.
Or don't. Who knows, maybe you're one of the lucky ones
who doesn't have to."

– Alan Wilson Watts

For my son Ariel,
whose innate knowledge
to follow his heart
remains an inspiration to me.

CONTENTS

PREFACE

Yes, yes. I know what that famous line is *supposed* to say! *"Let's KILL all the lawyers"*. The trouble is that people do conveniently misconstrue that notorious Shakespearean line to exacerbate the increasingly wayward perception held of the legal profession. And, I might add, it goes without saying that the general public do not need any more encouragement in the lawyer joke department. In my opinion – and I will let you know before we go any further that my opinion is far from humble – the time has come for we lawyers to consider a much-needed overhaul in the reputation department. An upgrade, if you will. *"So, how can this be achieved?"*, I hear you ask with sincere interest. Simple. Work needs to be done on lawyers' kiss-ability quotient. And stat.

"Kiss all the lawyers? Aren't they made of ice? Have you lost your mind?" In case you were wondering, that's the general public talking. With that kind of reaction, you may now rightly be wondering why then, as a 'country' lawyer and yoga teacher, would I be the most suitably qualified individual to lead this self-imposed, nigh impossible, charge? Well, aside from the yin and yang benefits I bring to the table, let me briefly mention my other important qualifications to put you at ease. I, for one like being kissed, and I sure don't need a PhD in kissing to tell you all about that.[1] They're soft, enjoyable, and there's that warm fuzzy feeling that goes with being kissed.

---

[1] *Note of caution about superiority complex of author: I thought it important to alleviate any early concerns you may have at the outset, in providing assurances that I am in no way superior to you with all my above-average kissing knowledge (despite lack of PhD on said topic). And just so we're clear, the extra letters after your name and the fact that you own two grey Armani suits doesn't make you superior to me. Well, do forgive me, I think I may have crossed the proverbial line making that last statement. My sense of humour is probably far superior to yours, but given that I'm not a judgemental person, I'll leave that for you to work out if you're up for the challenge. My life experiences so far have encouraged me to roll up my sleeves and amp up my daily fuzziness levels on my own, so I consider myself more than qualified to take charge of this diabolical situation. Solo! (Disclaimer: May need help from others.)*

Furthermore, being kissed is so much nicer than being 'killed' in Shakespearean fashion; painfully, with knives, in your BACK, no less! Ok, a bit dramatic, but I know you're all hearing me loud and clear as it seems to happen to our lot every day, even from our Very. Own. Colleagues, no less! (*audible gasps now heard by non-lawyer readers*).

Therefore, in the kiss versus kill stakes, you really do want to be the one on either end of the kissing. So, there you have it. I rest my case. The desired result has been indefeasibly proclaimed, by me. Kisses it is. With that handy piece of research settled by yours truly, you can now breathe a huge sigh of relief and know that you're in safe hands as I lead you on this covert operation. And I do mean covert, people! Once we have mastered this secret plan, the public won't know what's happened to us or them. There will be a grand outing of the new and improved Kissable Lawyer (KL v1.0) and all will be invited to gape in awe.

Even you will gape in awe.

I stand literally as Exhibit 'A'. The evidence of what you may have thought impossible. I've been on this crazy 'doing it differently' trip for a few years now, working up a tidy formula to raise the Kissability Index. Just ask my husband. He's turned eyerolling into an Olympic sport. He's my champion in more ways than he may ever know, particularly given that he's faithfully remained on this journey with me for the past 28 years.

The key is, if it weren't for all the valuable people who've shown up in my life, some of them posing as those 'teeth grittingly' persistent players, or as mere fleeting cameos (you all know who you are), I wouldn't be living the amazingly satisfying life I lead right now. Still in the practise of law. Yes, you read that right: Still. In. The. Practise. Of. Law.

I wanted to share from my own quirky perspective that it's *because* of the trouble-encrusted relationships in your life presenting themselves in neat little human packages, that life has substance. Once you unpack it all for what it really is, the grand prize is more kisses than you thought possible.

INTRODUCTION

I think we lawyers need kisses now more than ever, and those trusty old air kisses just aren't cutting it. With the picture of air kissing now firmly at the forefront of your minds, we need to engage in some wishful thinking and conjure up a delicious little recipe to get those air kisses to reach human skin. Real. Warm. Human. Skin. Yes, let's ponder this issue for a moment. How do we reach the desired kissable state? All the way from killable? Tall order. By the way, I would like you to carefully note that I'm not going for the whole 'irresistibly' kissable outcome. Irresistible? *Way* too far, people. I do have my limits!

To kick off, we need to start by taking a long, hard perusal of our good selves; to check out the chattels, if you will. We need to evaluate what we're working with here. What I have noticed, and the odds are favoured that you have too, is that the typical stereotypes slip into conversation whenever lawyers are mentioned. So much so, that at a gathering of non-lawyers, you catch yourself replying to the occupation question, saying "*Oh yes, I... 'er... am in sales*". Tell people you're a lawyer and you'll get the case of how their best friend was screwed over. Or you're regaled with that other gem that you are too expensive to talk to. Either way, you know it's preferable to feign some other job description to avoid being negatively pigeonholed.

By most accounts, we're top of the leader board in the professional unpopularity stakes, and for various reasons, which I think you'll agree need not be listed. According to that very reliable opinion of the ubiquitous person on the Clapham omnibus, we have been deemed exclusive members of the most despised profession in the world. And the cruellest part is, we worked our fingers to the bone to get our hands on that membership. The adjectives I've heard to describe certain individuals would make a gynaecologist blush.

Then, there's the cliché that has all lawyers *look* 'avariciously' the same in soulless grey Armani suits. That bothers me a *whole* lot, because: a) I just don't *do* grey; and, more importantly, b) I want to be known for strutting my stuff in my favourite leopard-print stilettos. The stilettos of *salvation,* I fondly call them.

Then of course, and probably most importantly, there are the somewhat gloomy stats I could recount on how the profession is suffering from varying forms of malady. Understandably, you probably don't want to use your valuable time reading, for the umpteenth time this week, that x% of us are staring aimlessly at the empty bottle of red and y% wonder why they didn't just accept that full-time position at [*insert favourite chocolate shop here*].

Whilst the dilemma we lawyers are facing are not exclusive to our profession, they are exacerbated by its adversarial nature and by the way we have been trained to deal with the issues put before us. We are trained to see both sides of an issue but must vigorously attain victory looking only at our client's side of the coin, no matter their ilk. How is that supposed to work in the real world? When doing so, we then address our opponent using the word 'friend'. *FRIEND?* Me thinks not! No wonder people think we have none. We all know that it's gone pear-shaped, and the only time I personally want to know more about these discouraging numbers is when they have decreased. Significantly.

In case you missed the memo, we are broadly being summarised by the outside world as cold, heartless, armour-plated, money-grabbing machines. Too many of us, in turn, have reacted by losing our zesty will to get up each day and face our own nemeses, the machines we have become. We now seem to have two battles: fighting for our clients, and more often than I'd like to see, we are fighting for ourselves. And that can, as I see it, only result in the death of a fine profession. As a good deal of us are figuring out how to embellish our resumes and turn the words 'money grabbing machine' into 'professional of intrinsically high value', it's clear we have work to do on ourselves and to the reputation of the profession as a whole.

So, let's get on with it and raise our Kissability Index, both for the benefit of ourselves and our clients. *"But how can this be done whilst we're wearing our shiny grey suits of Armani Armour?"*, you quite reasonably ask. Well, I'm happy to show you and then I'll have to kill you. This is, after all, a covert operation if you care to recall. Oh yes, hang on, I'm trying to avoid the whole killing bit, aren't I? Particularly as the term 'non-harm' is a principle I adhere to as best as my human capabilities will reasonably allow. Believe it or not, I am human.[2]

Seriously though, I've been fossicking around for answers to this very important question for around the past six or so years. I've studied some real science (not that imposter science) along with some now very reputable ancient philosophies. I've gathered up and collated additional credible research gleaned from other smart cookies such as academics, hypnotherapists, psychologists and other most duly qualified individuals all to help you gain ready access to the kissable creature you really are. You are just temporarily buried under some armour plating.

I will probably raise eyebrows as I am approaching this issue from such a light perspective (you can feel yours raising right now, can't you?) but being true to oneself is all part of the process. I was never the kind of girl that fit neatly into the mould. That was a bit of a burden for most of my life, but now I am very at ease being the odd one out, thank you for asking. And whilst I'm at it, you may notice that I tend to write with a sense of levity. But, it's here that I will be serious and say that if you feel at all like you are suffering from symptoms of depression, please seek out the appropriate medical professional for immediate assistance. My qualifications in that area are certainly lacking.

---

2 *You can spot those aliens a mile away, they always drool in those sci-fi movies, and you can readily see that I'm not a drooler... spoils the lipstick.*

The point is, the way is light. It's easy. That's how it's meant to be. I really do want you to have fun with this. I *already* have fun with this. The principles I am guiding you through work for me. I have purpose and I understand why I am here and, for the most part, what I am doing.[3] That in itself, is worthwhile. Besides, a little frivolity never hurt anyone. Not anyone I know personally anyway. Oh, and why do I want to keep this all secret until the grand unveiling? I am joking, of course. Share the information I'm imparting with as many people as you can. I guarantee it cannot make things worse. Indeed, it may just be the kiss someone was waiting for.

So, if the way I get up and start my day has a positive impact on how I speak to my secretary in the morning, then you just might want a slice of this breakfast. And in the words of Meghan Trainor... "*If I was you I'd wanna be me to*". And so you know, I do like breaking into song now and then.

Disclaimer: No leopards were harmed in the discussion or wearing of my preferred legal attire.

---

3 *Provided I have a list. At my age, I need lists.*

PART
I

I know you're
in there

CHAPTER

1

So you decided to become a lawyer?

Why on Earth did you decide to do that?

- Well, first and foremost, we can agree that lawyers are highly intelligent. That's a great quality to showcase.

- Then, of course, lawyers are instrumental in lobbying for public change and thwarting that wretched beast injustice. That's honourable.

- And don't forget, your mother told you that you were very good at arguing. Why not count that as a shoo-in toward your career success?

- And a dream of a career in law would not be complete without giving one of those television courtroom dramas a solid mention. You saw those litigators in full flight. You fantasized about pacing the courtroom. In your Armani suit. You saw yourself call surprise witness after surprise witness, to the awe of the jury. You saw your name in lights. You could revel in that glory.

And the legends go on.

A grand and well thought out decision! You sweat it out through secondary school to get a score high enough to get into the most prestigious university. Then woo hoo! All those years in law school, traineeship way behind you, visions of 'Lawyerup' on your number plate, corner office complete with views, and most important of all, The Swivel Chair. There is nothing in life that oozes success as much as the drama created by the *swoosh* of The Swivel Chair. Picture this: Imposingly high back of chair faces door. Nervous employee enters. *Swooosh!* A full 180 degrees of swivel precisely executed. Eyes lock with said employee. Tension mounts. "*Order me up two pieces of sushi! Hold the wasabi!!*", you dictate. Employee nervously backs out. You've made it! Everyone's gonna LOVE me! I will be SOOOOO kissable.

Wrong!

A little time passes, and in walks Rude Awakening, that nasty fellow. Old Mr A presents you with the grand realisation that your brilliant career is not much more than working insane hours for little extra reward, dealing with difficult people on both sides of the fence. Then that clever brain of yours, that worked so hard to get to this point, is turning to mush from doing rote court filing and making cups of tea, all the while those above you shade your sunlight. And despite your mother's assurances, your gifted arguing skills don't mean much in this setting because no-one is listening. It's deflating and downright deceiving. You now align yourself with the phrase, "*suck it up princess!*" You then spend the next X number of years embellishing your worth in ways that would make said mother blush, all to get noticed and to find yourself a place on the 'team'. There are only 'I's' in this team, people! By this stage, you have lost yourself, even though by all accounts you are now 'somebody'. But something got lost in that process.

It was you.

I saw how easily that scenario happened. Even though I did not enter law in quite the same way I set out above, I can say that despite my path in, the outcome was still similar. I became a lawyer quite by accident, but I have since discovered that nothing – I repeat, *nothing* – ever happens by accident. Even the accidents.

I came into law in a roundabout way. The short story is that I approached a local law firm with an employment issue I had with a previous employer. The lawyer told me that I could take the matter further, but that would be of no use seeing I suffered no loss. "*What do you mean no loss?*" says I with mouth agape. You see, the firm offered me a job, so I hadn't suffered any loss (oh and they didn't charge me for the legal advice).

See the path being mapped out here? Destiny unfolding. Bad experience turned into good experience. Clouds, linings, all that stuff. Look out career in Law, here I come!

Sometime later, that same law firm I was working for was acquired by a lawyer from the city who was seeking a sea change. He, at the time, was not all that familiar with the nuances of a small, private, legal practice. He saw my potential and encouraged me to apply to go through law school. I had high ideals at the start. I would help people. I am a person. I like being helped. "*It is what I'll do*," I declared (hands on hips with cape flapping in the breeze)! I managed to accomplish this task via correspondence, with a toddler and a full-time job as a paralegal in the law firm to contend with.[4] Very early mornings, weekends and evenings no longer my own. Sound familiar?

I worked in, and am now a Partner of that small firm. The hours are better than those of my city colleagues, and the work is generally rewarding. But being a Partner, like any small business owner, aside from getting on with it and earning a living, you have an array of

---

4 *Not set out in order of difficulty, so as to protect the innocent.*

other treasures to deal with each day, like staff, administration, that funny little creature called accounting, and the seemingly endlessly changing regulation imposed on us by our regulatory bodies.

They didn't teach us that in law school.

I then discovered that due to many other, including aforementioned pressures, we must watch out for serious health concerns that can arise. First, our job description focuses on the use of our clever grey matter and disregards the rest of our person. We find ourselves sitting all day, which is not, I'm reliably informed, a remedial form of relaxation. Then there is the stress factor-y. A typical day can often lead to us staring at a computer screen awaiting the most creative of words to flow, only to be distracted by some well-meaning opponent telephoning us to question our costs. Oh, and then you realise you only have one week left to get your last Compulsory Professional Development point and you're looking everywhere for one hour of Professional Skills, of all topics. Don't get me started.

This stuff all happens without a client even being in sight. You know the feeling. The shoulders start tensing up around your ears and by the end of the day, you're looking for your happy place at the bottom of that nice bottle of red. It's justified, you say; after all, no-one but us lawyers (and that calming, tasty bottle of red) understands the complexities attached to our profession.

Then of course, there is that other minor detail; the reason that we practise. The clients. They don't come bearing chocolates, people! They come with problems. Some really, really difficult problems that can set your head spinning in their seeming insurmountability. We then must absorb and understand their problem and explain it to a few other people, like opposing Counsel and Judges, in the hope that they too understand our client's plight. But invariably there are those who do not, or choose not to, given that the nature of our work is intrinsically centred in conflict, and that we have been trained to act with a very special form of righteousness.

So, on with the fight. I explain my client's position, putting best stilettoed foot forward, even throw in some sound legal argument for good measure. And what do I often receive for my trouble? Angry retorts, expletives, and attacks of a personal nature that I won't repeat here, despite said attacks being against our practising rules. These 'conversations' can often be bitter, pointed and in my view, soulless. I would sit and ponder after hanging up the phone on such 'meaningful' banter, and begin to ask myself questions like: Do they have kids, like me? Did they have to think about what's for dinner and get home to "*No, not risotto again!*" This was my turning point. I questioned, how do I stay swimming with the sharks but not get eaten? How can I wear that Suit differently? Can I wear leopard print? Does it *really* have to be Armani?

So many important questions, so little time.

I was once labelled 'Ice Queen' by one of my opposing clients. Hmmm, 'IQ'. Had a nice ring to it. That's how it's supposed to be, isn't it? Vigorously defend and all. Made of ice. Heart frozen over. Those barbs can't penetrate this ice, baby! But no. Speak to the hand! I decided categorically then and there, that's not who I wanted to be known as. Not at all.

Whilst pondering the meaning of all this, another little 'accident' happened to me. This one really did hurt. Again, I say, things don't happen by accident, but in my case yoga did, in the literal sense. And it wasn't pretty. There I was, teetering along the main street in my favourite leopard-print heels, when out of nowhere at the pedestrian crossing, *thud!* Down I went before stunned onlookers, dignity and all. Just imagine me, suited up in the middle of the crossing on my hands and knees, wishing those stripes would open and swallow me whole. Quite funny in hindsight, but totally embarrassing then! No more Zumba for me, my knees were in no condition to help me shake that 'thang' anymore. So, off to the chiropractor I went. He dryly suggested I try yoga as therapy for both my bruised ego and knees, which in turn was met with my audible eye rolls and my inaudible mutters of *"yeah, that'll be like watching paint dry..."* as I limped away. You know where I'm coming from, right? *Boring...*

That memorable event happened some years ago and, happily, my knees and ego are much better, thank you for asking. The point is, yoga surprised me. So much so, that I am now a registered Yoga Teacher. Here I was, thinking yoga was all about sitting in lotus position chanting "om".[5] Remarkably, I found yoga to be much more than that. Steeped in traditional Indian and Himalayan philosophies dating back to the beginning of known civilization, the science of yoga – yes, you heard right, science – is all about caring for your body, mind and breath through a combination of physical movements, breathing techniques and soothing mindful meditation.

I discovered the many benefits from practising yoga really worked for me. I was feeling great. But I'm not here to talk about yoga in the truest sense. My painful meeting with yoga opened a unique portal to a field of knowledge that changed my entire approach to life. I was on a brand-new grand adventure. The Ice Queen would be melted once and for all. A new identity was on the way.

As I delved deeper into this discovery, what stood out for me most was that I encountered many other professionals, including some lawyers, who felt just like me. The trouble was, after this lot became privy to the good stuff, realising how easily life can become a kissable wonder-trip, they slipped quietly out of that barbwire-edged corporate world to bask in that relatively serene existence on the 'other side' where all the people are living a most kissable existence.

---

5 *I know, you're surprised. I am wrong occasionally.*

What I want to see is for us to is move the border so that we, too, live on the kissable side all the while using the skills we worked so hard to achieve. Society needs clever brains. I want to show you that starting with some small shifts in your daily perspective, you can and will make a marked difference in your life, and in the lives of others. It is my hope this would result in a vital shift in the perception of our profession and of the place it should hold in our society. Some of my fabulous colleagues working in this area are calling this shift a paradigm shift. Powerful!

The experiences I've had since my leopard-print shoes betrayed me, have opened a door to a whole new way of life, and way of thinking for me. My perception on life has shifted. Bless those shoes. To paraphrase the insightful words of the amazing Socrates, I am writing this to impart some knowledge, but only to the extent of offering you an opportunity to think about your life from a different perspective. It's all in your perspective.

What we need to do is go within. Penetrate the Suit of Armour and take a peek inside. I, for one, want to be loved for what I do. Well, even being *liked* for what I do would be a great start. Let's change the reputation of our profession from that of ballbreakers to icebreakers. Let all the law students exclaim, *"I'll have one of what she's having!"*[6] and be able to deliver on that promise.

---

6 *Insert standard boilerplate clause here. You know, he equals she equals them. To clarify: she, he, you, me or them can be plural or singular. I, for one am plural, I'm a Gemini. But that's another story.*

CHAPTER

2

Putting a chink
in the armour

Great! You've reached this point.

I know you have, and you know you have.

You're now looking over your shoulder and thinking about how creepy that sounds.

For all you contract lawyers out there, I think we'll just wink and agree that a little estoppel has just arisen. Exciting times. Importantly, I'll take it that we're all on the same page and agree that this scary state of affairs needs to change. As you are still reading this book, I'll invite you to climb aboard this discovery chariot. Yes, yes! With your armour on. I will escort you on an exciting quest. Don't panic. You can still wear the Suit for the time being. After all, you've undergone some rigorous training to keep it in place. In any event, I am not about to change you into something unrecognisable. I have no power or desire whatsoever to change you at all in fact. You will remain perfectly you. At all times. Intact.

As leader[7] of this little expedition, I will reveal all. You have been obscured by that shiny metal Suit for far too long. I'm going to dutifully get my pointer out and tap on some signposts emblazoned with the directions you may choose to take. You will still have your law degree, it's how you will use it in the future that is quite probably up for the challenge, should you so elect. You just may conclude there is a different way of looking at how this life is all supposed to pan out. You may even end up choosing to disassemble that armour a little piece at a time. It's all up to you, no-one else. This is a personal trek, a conversation between you and the Suit which, by its very nature, means that it's not a competition.

So, what's my grand plan to sneak you past the gatekeeper of that impenetrable metaphorical Suit of Armour? You went to law school to learn the hell how to put that armour on. It took work! Years of work to get it to the state it's in. Ironclad. Immovable. Stubborn. No wonder affection remains elusive. Affection? Emotion? Lawyers aren't trained in emotion, there was no Emotion 101 in law school. Pfft! No emotion to be seen here... move along!

You may now have an inkling that what I'm saying is, you can't get kisses if you are engulfed by the Suit, no matter whether it's very shiny or even diamond-encrusted. The amount of money you throw at it doesn't help either, so get that thought right out of your head. The reason is, that when you slip into that Suit you become cold and hard (like the facts), inVINCEable and at times, even downright discourteous! The moment it goes on, you forget that you kissed your mother last night (sans Suit, of course), or even the fact you have a mother. After all, YOU didn't need another human to bring you into existence, because it's all about you. You

7 *I know, you're shocked, you hadn't realised until now that I am a woman of many talents, including expedition leader, in heels. Another fine example of how you can do anything you want to in this life.*

will conquer the world for your client. Take no prisoners to secure that vital win. I rest my case, your Honour! Evil Suit.

At first this is great fun. The power. Your friends are so very impressed. They must shade their eyes when they see you in that Suit. My god, you are GLORIOUS! But after a while it's hard to keep the polish up. It's exhausting! Then the shine starts wearing off (dictate note to secretary to order self-shining Suit – surely, they've invented one of those by now, haven't they?). Uh oh, no kisses for you! You simply cannot kiss someone in a full Suit of Armour, even if it is Armani. You start missing out on those kisses and you wonder how it came to this. There you are, looking in the mirror, wondering what the *bleep* happened to your life. You worked hard. You did everything right. Didn't you?

Now let's take a closer look at these things called kisses. How can they solve this little dilemma?

Well, at one point, I thought I had discovered some impressive research to support my theory that those soft, lovely kisses are the secret to happiness. Let's face it, India celebrates a Happy Kiss Day and then, of course, you have July 6 every year which is International Kissing Day. It's international, people, so it must be very important! Whilst I thought I could build a good case that kisses are right up there as the pinnacle of happiness, sadly, more reliable research says that chocolate is the real winner in the happiness stakes.

Now, despite that traitor chocolate's winning smile, I'm not going to let some tediously accurate research ruin a perfectly good story. Especially as I really don't want to be given chocolates as a token of my client's appreciation. Not good for the thighs/bellies or whatever other body part your consumption of chocolate is attracted to. Mmmm... chocolate. Anyway, according to that research, to be truly happy, I'd best order those M&Ms to "*get into the bowl"*. Then while I'm at it, bowl in hand, I'll just hop on eBay and buy those sparkly earrings I've always wanted. There I'll sit, feet up, munching away, picturing myself gleaming in those earrings I just bought. My friends will be so jealous. That right there, my friends, and I do mean friends in the warmest possible way, is one perfectly clichéd picture of happiness.

Sadly, though, the key to finding the happiest place on Earth is not within the delicious chocolate centres of M&Ms, or even in the wearing of those earrings, which are now at the bottom of in my handbag, never again to see the light of day! Whilst fun at the time (except for foraging in said handbag for earrings, which equals the exact opposite of fun) these are all transient treats and have an expiry date in terms of their pleasure-giving capabilities. Happiness, as you are no doubt all rather aware, does not come from external gratification. It comes from within your good selves.

Yes, I assure you, it is in there.

Given that my personal research (and we can now clearly see that my personal research is all that counts in this story) reveals chocolate as falling flat in its enjoyment longevity, I'll now rely heavily upon the second-place getter, the runner-up: Kisses, as my go-to evidence. In any event, I've heard that the science of kisses can offer us a useful clue as to where we can begin this quest (or I could be just making that part up, but nonetheless, you will see it makes a great segue).

Kisses, I think we might all readily agree, have generally been deemed team players in the love[8] game. Simple concepts like love have been the subject of conjecture for eons, and it remains a difficult sentiment to define. Interestingly, the question *"What is Love?"*, was the top Google search for 2012, that elusive little puppy.

---

8 *Did you like that? Smooooth. Eased right in! They told me I couldn't talk to lawyers about love right up. Too scary. You know, especially since you haven't had formal training in the emotional stuff and all.*

And just because that question hasn't ranked again, doesn't mean people have figured it out. Think about it. The year 2012 was the year everyone thought the world was going to end.

Yes, there really are people out there that believed that! I know without even asking that you would not have believed that nonsense, because we very sensible lawyers need cold hard facts. Cold and hard. That's ~~who we are~~ what we need before we can be convinced of anything, really. Moving on, it makes complete sense to me then, that if people were thinking the planet was going to explode, then they were quite entitled to make one last ditch effort to get to the bottom of it all. We do know that love is as old as the hills and, as a result of being in vogue for a very long time, has a rather good reputation. *"What is it, and how do I get some?"*, you ask. Not so fast, you eager beavers (*wink*).

Love. It can make us feel like we're floating on air, but it can also be devastating. It's a fickle beast. What I'm talking about in this instance, is being *in* love. That romantic business. Whilst that kind of love can bring you great happiness, it can also make you wish you had never met it. Ever. The kind of love I'm referring to is different. It's a deeper, fuzzier emotion (there's that word again) that only exists on the positive end of the scale. It's often described as a feeling, or just a thing you give but don't expect anything in return. Think soft kisses, and multiply by a whole lot. You can put the calculator away.

Let me put it another way.

If you picture kisses as being a form of appreciation, think then that the love I'm referring to represents an overwhelming form of appreciation. It's literally heart-warming. It doesn't come or go. It just is. Pretty deep stuff. But sounds mighty fine, doesn't it? Love. Just there. Free. For you. All the time.

What we need to do to find such a mysterious creature is go within, and warm up that icicle heart. We won't just chink that armour, we'll melt it from the inside out. Bingo! That's it. Case closed. Love is all you need. (I'll have the Beatles LP at the ready.)

Note: Before you start thinking about it, no, money can't buy you love! Please refer to aforementioned Beatles LP.

Who's really lurking beneath the suit?

The challenge is, how to get that '*crazy little thing called love*' to melt the Suit (all you IP lawyers, please advise on whether credit to Queen necessary here). First, we need to take a step back and check you out. We need to discover who is really lurking in there, carefully concealed beneath the Suit of glory? I will interject a little philosophy here, if you don't mind, as I ask that very personal question... "Who *are* you?"

Let's do a little run-though. When you meet people, you say, "*Hi, I'm Bob*". Well, not if you're not Bob, but we'll just use the name Bob because it starts with a 'B' and ends with a 'b', and I like its symmetry. No offence intended to any other names. So, fine, if you're Bob. But who is Bob? Bob is not really who Bob thinks Bob is. That's just Bob's label, used so Bob knows you're referring to him when you're saying, "*Bob, where the hell's the brief?*". From that, you can deduce further that Bob's day job is a lawyer. But that also does not define him. I need you to really absorb that. You may introduce yourself as a lawyer, but that's not who you are. Father, brother, clarinet player – those are labels. They are not *you*.

Let's take a further step back, a deeper look at you beneath the armour and the labels. Conveniently, I have *hand* drawn a diagram. Please! Oh, do sit down! I really do NOT need all this applause... oh dear!

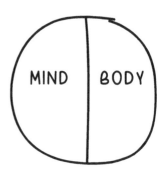

This is you.
If you were a circle.

Imagine I have a pointer. I am now making big important circles all around the diagram. This is you. Mind and body. I now have my pointer firmly tapping on the left side of the diagram. Your mind, particularly in your day job as a lawyer, is the most important tool you *think* you have. Law, by nature, requires you to spend a good deal of time in your head. It's a proper workout. Mental gymnastics sometimes. Often, so much so, that you don't have any time at all left, or you are too exhausted to look after the rest of you.

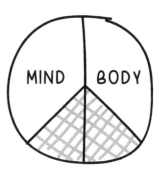

The missing peace
(see what I did there?)

Then *tap tap* on the right side of the diagram, is your body. Let me have a little chat to you about the chocolate you've been eating (that traitor chocolate). I can see some of you conscientious peeps like to keep that body of yours all svelte too. If you're one of those individuals, then good job! Fit body, fit mind. The complete package.

But guess what? Ta-da! If you thought that was all you had under the Suit, then think again. (*Author amends diagram and taps rapidly at hatched area*) Okay, okay, I'll put the pointer down! This, my friends, represents you. If, that is, you had all your bits.

Well then, *"What is this missing peace? How do I get some?"* All great questions, which I assure you will be answered in the fullness of time. If you can think creatively, just imagine, if you will, doing your day job with a sense of peace. How would that feel? *"Too big a challenge"*, you say. *"Fantasy!"*, says another. *"Impossible!"*, I hear from the gentleman in the back row.

Understandable reactions.

Peace is missing for a good number of us lawyers primarily due to the lack of any realistically sustainable work-life balance. We work excessive hours to meet the demands of our high-stress profession. Again, added to this is that the very nature of our work is based in conflict. How can we maintain peace and operate in situations of conflict at the same time? Palpitations are no doubt arising in your chest just at the mere thought of what we go through each day. Yes, your heart has something to do with this conundrum.

In my mission to help you find the missing peace, let me share something that you will relate to right away. A lawyer's job is not to know all the law. As we all know too well, the law is never in one place at one time, it's a moveable feast. Our job as lawyers is to find it and apply it to the factual circumstances before us. In a similar fashion, someone trained in a peaceful way of being, like a yogi, has the task of finding that elusive inner peace by utilising certain proven methods to restore it. On both accounts, it's a continual process. The law moves, and peace moves. As you probably know by now, I'm across both those tasks and I am delighted to light the way on the latter.

I should point out here that this peace everyone looks for is integrally connected to love. The love I refer to is the second type I discussed earlier. Of the heart-warming variety. After all, if you have a warm heart, I have discovered that no-one can call you Ice Queen. Mostly because, by definition, there is a part of you that is warm (so scientific of me).

Let's for now think of love as our kryptonite in this game. Arch enemy of the super Armani Suit of Armour. I do need to take it deeper again. Here you will meet the part of you that makes it easier to help locate and maintain the peace. The place where love resides. Now, stick with me and I'll take you on a little trip. Yes, you'll probably think I'm trippin' already, but let me remind you again there is solid science backing me up, along with tales of my own expedition from Ice Queen to Queen of Hearts, offering some real-life encouragement.

Now pack up your ice picks. We're going on a little journey[9] beneath the Suit of Glory to meet the treasure inside that is you, the one we will now cheekily refer to as 'The Whole Circle'.

Peace out.

---

9 *It'd be really cool to do this all Fantastic Voyage style and shrink you inside a mini submarine, but, and I know you must be shocked at this, I am not at all skilled in the art of shrinking people... now laundry, that's another story, but we won't go there.*

PART
II

Sealed Section

WARNING:
contains esoteric language
and mind-opening themes

Sceptical Reader

May also contain nuts!!!

Me
*clears throat, takes deep
breath and smooths skirt*

Now, why don't we just,
give peace a chance?

Caveat Emptor

I must unashamedly let you know right here, that when first contemplating the message I wanted to deliver you all in this book, the inclusion of content of the nature of this Part II terrified me. For a moment. Maybe two moments.

To check in on whether I'd gone completely mad, I consulted some of my more open-minded colleagues on the matter. I assure you they do exist. They gently nudged me into questioning whether my thinking suited my target audience (equally terrified for me, I suspect). That's why I'm giving you the option of reading it, or not. It's entirely your choice.[10]

Before you make your choice, I would like you to consider my argument on why you might choose for the affirmative.

Before I launched into the reputational space of no return, I decided to test the waters. I'd dip my toe in to see whether or not it froze over, given the prior sentiment of my colleagues. In imposing my concept of existence onto others, I figured humour works best, so I started posting fun messages with deeper meaning about life's journey on social media. What I found were numerous lawyers out there in cyberspace strangely curious about the work I was doing. My toe felt warm. Many of them were finding their day job traumatic and found some solace in the messages I was offering. Who wants to go to work to feel traumatised? Who wins that one? How can a person who feels internal conflict with the work they spent years training for, head out each day with a smile and tell you how to resolve yours?

---

10 *Choice. It's a powerful thing. You have it. What I've exposed you to there is the noun. It's also a verb, a doing word. It's your choice whether you use your choice. Believe me when I tell you it's a choice word that you could choose to use more often, if you so choose.*

That many lawyers sent me private messages seeking a better way, seemed to me that they're afraid to 'come out'. Afraid to stand up and practise law in a way that doesn't fit the stereotype. When one of my colleagues learned of my approach, he whispered that he, too, relies on his esoteric ways. But he keeps them locked securely in his "crystal closet", for fear of ridicule. It saddens me greatly to know there are those of you out there who cannot be true to your good selves and carry out your day job all at the same time. That, in my opinion, is soul destroying, and not who you are meant to be.

I then set off on another quest looking into the ready availability of wellness programs for lawyers. To get a flavour for it. My starting point was with the governing bodies of our profession here in Australia. There wasn't much really. Nothing you could really sink your teeth into. Nothing that rang a winning bell for me, saying what I wanted to hear, to the tune of: *"This is the answer. You'll feel better now."*.

It felt like I'd have to wipe the dust off some of the publications that offered up general remedial advice divided into headings that looked something like this: get enough sleep; eat properly; exercise; drink lots of water; speak to someone (like your supervisor, who was probably the one stressing you out in the first place) and, 'go meditate'.

Go meditate? *Rrrright...* My heart sank.

Not how or why to meditate. Just do it. I mean, really? You're talking to lawyers.

It bothered me somewhat that there was no further guidance on that point and that these were obligatory words that, whilst sounding well thought out, like lawyers have it all together, had no real substance. I wondered right then if anyone really knew what meditation meant. It was there I felt it appropriate to explore the possibility of whether there was a general understanding in our industry of what, at an elemental level, that creature called meditation really is. Yes, it makes us feel calm. Yes, it creates peace. Yes, there are many great benefits to meditation and I strongly advocate for it.

But without knowing who YOU really are, if and when you have reached that deep level of meditation, it's not much help to you in the day-to-day grind of it all. More than that, if you're awesome at meditating, you might find yourself wanting to stay 'in the zone' more than you want to really get out there with a passion to become engaged in the daily drudgery. 'The zone' is a cool place. But not understanding who you really are, and why you're in the messes you get yourself in, you're missing the point entirely. When you get that, you can live and grind in 'the zone' all at the same time. Grinding in the zone. Now that's emulsification.

This debacle drove me to the unavoidable conclusion that I cannot NOT tell you what I know.

With those lovely legal words, *ipso facto*, being cleverly used by me, it's because of what I'm going to share with you that has made me the person I am now. I now know who I am. In that knowing is great power. The power not to be afraid of judgement. The power to be calmer in the drama. The power in knowing that all is perfect and exactly how it should be. I am at peace. As much as a human can be, that is. The I, who is at great peace with herself, can now step into this arena without her sword and shield as protection. She must live her purpose.

This Part II is meant for those of you that have reached the end of your proverbial tether. Those of you who are ready to take on a new perspective in considering the importance of internal conflict. You know something is off. The way you're living your life is just not right for you any longer. You are the ones who feel it. You get it. I therefore felt it of vital importance to take this to a deeper level and introduce you to your truest self. That part of you that's now saying: "*I want more from all of this.*"

I write this Part from a place guided by my heart, which you will later see is as equally representative of the real me as my mind. I will again say that my view of the world and my purpose in it took on a whole new meaning the day I discovered yoga. Yoga, I learned, represented one of the many views on life's substance. But as I delved deeper, I suddenly saw things in the way you do when your plane is coming into land and you can just make out the teeny tiny cars and houses below. My vantage point gave me the big picture. The whole shebang. It showed me how perspective changes everything. It was a powerful revelation.

None of this information is new. It's been around in various forms practised by people such as shamans, Zen masters and yogis, to name a few, for as long as time itself. We see 'alternative' medicine gaining strength in its potent healing abilities. I say that modern medicine is, in fact, the alternative. What I see for the legal profession in dealing with human conflict, has been traditionally used by shamans. They have expressed brilliant methods in healing relationship conflict. It comes from understanding at a fundamental level who we are before we can know how to reach that point again. When you think about it, not much of anything is really that new. It's mostly just tried principles applied to a different perspective. It springboards evolution. The way forward is to apply alternative laws to the facts in the knowledge that the adversarial way in which we've been practising, sucks. Let's see how we can change outcomes for the betterment of all.

This part explains the nature of we humans at a deeper level than our bare bones. The 'hu?' in humanity.

In case you haven't noticed, in making life choices we always move toward doing that which feels good. We inherently want to feel better. When you appreciate that the fundamental component of you is the 'good' you are indeed looking for, then you will understand that my dear friend chocolate will never cut it in the enduring happiness stakes.

If any of you think I have lost my mind, to that I say a resounding "*yes!*". But not in the way you or I would ordinarily think. My mind, or part thereof, is just a tool I use to accomplish the tasks I need to carry out for the reason I exist on this planet. My mind is not really who I am. It's an integral part of my humanness, but it is not me. Or you.

This Part explains how you came to be perfection incarnate. It sheds light on why you do the things you do that appear less than perfect, and how you can return to your innate state with the benefit of understanding the reasons behind your actions. We no longer have to sit in a cave and meditate for years on end to discover how to feel better, or to discover who we are. It is staring us in the face and it is called life.

Are you ready? I hope so. This is the fun part.

CHAPTER

1

You thrill seeker

Good! You chose to at least take a peek! I like it that you are freely exercising your power of choice. But further to my caveat above, I warn you: if you continue, you will read things that can't be unread...

Okay, I still have you. I, being the invariable me that I am, have now deemed you to be one of the 'insiders' as you embark on a journey that will take you to a place Deep... Inside... The... Suit. I'd love to say about now, that I am taking you *"where no-one has gone before"* Star-Trek style, but I have to disappoint you I'm afraid, and confess that loads of people have taken this little trip. Anyway, I am certain it remains unchartered territory for most of you, else you wouldn't be reading this.

Before you choose to proceed further, I want to assure you that I have purposefully separated this Part II because the content of the book can stand well on its own without this information. You do not need the fun stories and otherwise interesting information set out in this Part in order to understand the concepts and implement the practical strategies I convey in Part III. However, and this is a BIG however, I remind you again that the central reason behind my motivation for writing this Part is because I have found there is a type of 'causal link' missing in most mainstream literature out there on the real reasons we do the things we humans do. Even though, I will now happily say, this gap in information is rapidly shrinking in direct proportion to the greater scientific evidentiary support for the ancient philosophies to which I refer.

For instance, most of us in this modern world have been rightly told how stress is bad for us. We are then provided with sound remedial methods on how to de-stress. As I noted previously, "*Go meditate*", they say. "*You'll feel better*", they say. Why? Well, you are told there are health benefits, and you will feel centred. Breathe this way and that. Sit on a cushion. Count to 10. Hold your breath. Don't turn blue. No, don't let the dog in.

Do that in all the right order and you will de-stress because someone said so.[11] But then you let the dog in. All your good leg crossing, breath counting, peace-inducing moments shattered. Right there. *Why can't I do this right?*, you wonder. And no, it wasn't the dog's fault. Missing from the daily repertoire in this illustration is the fundamental element as to why you will, or why you will not, reach your happy place.

Now I know you all love a good causal link. It connects the cause and effect. It's the because in all our legal why's. It's the honey in our tea. Need I go on about its importance. But I'm guessing that the *type* of causal link to which I'm referring has been missing all too long because it's too 'way out there' for some good folks to consider. Remember back in the day when you had to physically go back to the office to call someone from a telephone that had a dial? Now, you can talk into your watch whilst cars are driving themselves. Open minds are clearly the order of the 21st century. And an open mind is what you will need to understand who you really are.

---

11 *Mind you, I don't have anything against someone saying something is so. After all, we humans once believed the world was flat until the global movement got around.*

Let's go back to describing a human and you'll see what I mean. Not like the Bob example I provided earlier. Bob's a member of one of those expensive Golf Clubs and a Porsche owner. That Bob certainly knows who he is. Rich. He's got it sorted and has certificates to prove it. Most people are comfortable dealing with this physically quantifiable type of situation. I can touch it. I can see it, therefore it's real.

Now let's look at humans in another way. They laugh. They cry. They have squishy bits that seal over when cut open. Their hearts beat, and their brains think (some of them anyway). How do they manage to do all this?

It wasn't enough for me to accept that it's just the way it is. Of course, we have the Darwinian theory of evolution, which says life commenced from a puddle-bound amoebic source of consciousness. I'm now imagining how I could evolve from a fish, and wonder why the good folk of evolution didn't leave in my underwater breathing skills. I might then enjoy swimming a little more than I do.

I digress. From my perspective, I simply wanted to know why it was that I couldn't just stop eating chocolate when I *knew* I wanted to. I mean, who was I always arguing with in my own head? I had to uncover these great mysteries because I felt there was more to me than met my eyes.

Whilst I got the underlying hint that there was a good deal more to this thing we all call life when I was quite young (you probably have that sense too, else you would not be reading this), the major shift happened when yoga and I first met. This is not all about yoga, however; again, yoga was just my gateway to a whole new world (it was like I took an 'Aladdinesque' magic carpet ride). On this plush pile incursion, I have been exposed to some very simple methods of self-discovery. Simple ways to help me fill in the blanks, to answering the questions I had about life and what the hell it's all about. After I got to the bottom of who I was, I was then able to use those tools to help my clients, some of whom were experiencing critical periods in their lives and needed some direction on how to get through the emotional turmoil.

Now, I want to share my understanding of it all with my colleagues as I verily believe that to understand your humanness is to understand why you, and everyone else, are doing what they are doing. And to have that insight makes your day job that whole lot more enjoyable as you begin to work within our adversarial system in this light.

Now you may have heard of the law of attraction. It is a fairly mainstream concept these days and is showcased in books like *The Secret*. Its philosophy, very simply put, is that if you're in a happy place with happy intentions, you will attract happy things.[12] Things such as our friend chocolate. This attraction business is really all about energy. Energy is the word of the moment here.

I first came across that notion and had the good fortune to be exposed to that type of life-changing writing in Florence Scovel Schinn's *The Game of Life and How to Play It*. I found this book in 1996, 'accidentally'. I cannot remember how it came across my path. That book was written in 1925. There was no Internet at my disposal then and I did not really frequent libraries. After reading that book, I was profoundly changed. It resonated with me and I *knew* there was sound reasoning in its writings. That was the beginning. The initial spark.

It was then during my yoga teacher training that my life direction again changed markedly. During my studies, I delved into diverse readings, which inspired an interest in me that I again *knew* was there all along. The 'knowing', as I like to call it, that we all have

---

12 Disclaimer: *people found out that there is way more to the law of attraction than they were sold. Nonetheless, the law of attraction is a real 'thing'. It's just not as simple as it's portrayed. I'll tell you all about it another day.*

can be also called your intuition. In particular, I read an article on a yoga website that referred to a place called 'home' (where we go after leaving our physical bodies). Well that was it. Full body tingles happened there and then. I knew I had hit the jackpot, I was in my happy place. I needed more information and I needed it right away. As a result, I have been reading and analysing metaphysical-type writings and philosophies like crazy.

A good deal of the work I've read is based in science such as quantum physics, which offers up proven theories on energy and its tricky behaviour. Some of the works are also written by such duly qualified peeps as hypnotherapists, psychologists, academics and the like. There is a wealth of fabulous literature available helping people find a better way, from many perspectives. All great stuff and if you look closely you will find consistent underlying threads.

As you may also find, some philosophies resonated with me, some did not. I reason that if I share with others what I have read and some of the life-changing insights I've gained, then I may just help you find your tingles and start breaking through that armour.

So here you are, you have read this far. I'm tickled because it could just be that you are curious about how I got to the happy place I find myself in. I'm telling a different story about how you can make that elusive peace an every-day part of your law-practising existence, I think. I go where angels fear to tread. That's not true at all, angels aren't scared of anything. And before I freak you out completely, I'm not at all religious and want you to rest assured that I am only positing this information for you to consider, for you have probably tried other ways of reaching your happy place that just haven't cut the proverbial mustard. Hang on tight, because I'm going to take you on a little trip, and as Eminem[13] says:

---

13 *Note about strange musical tastes of author: Yes, I am an Eminem fan; mostly of his popular stuff though (just like the New Zealand government, I hear). Shocked readers revolt: "That's not very Zen!" but I beg to differ. There are some great human messages in*

"...we need a little controversy".

My research has so far led me to draw some personal conclusions on some very provocative ideas such as: why are we here? On life and death generally, and what happens to us when we die. Some of you might find that the concepts I've discovered in that research as being pretty far-fetched. But as I pointed out earlier, that's okay with me. I do urge you, however, if you have the slightest inkling that something greater than yourself exists out there, other than God, Allah or whatever other deity you follow in the most traditional of senses, then I may just have something for you to ponder. I share my views with you because it has become a part of my 'knowing' that it is my job to do so. In other words, to again quote the great Marshall Bruce Mathers III: *"This looks like a job for me ..."*

---

his lyrics, and we all need good human messages, and to give credit to the songwriter of those messages *wink*.

CHAPTER

2

In the beginning...

Sounds rather biblical, doesn't it? Don't worry, as I've previously mentioned, organised religion is not for me. Trust me when I say that despite being encouraged (let's call it bribed, shall we?) to attend a variety of churches in my tender years, nothing could convince me that the sound of thunder was just God moving 'his' piano. This is largely because no-one could give me a reasonable explanation for thunder's good friend lightning. I mean God wouldn't need to use flash photography, would 'he' – remember, after all 'he', according to all sources is light, people! Not saying that if you do believe in the good Lord that you are wrong, I just need you to explain to me why we must have lightning. I'm terrified of it! Jokes aside, religion does have its good points and I do respect all religions for the core messages they deliver. It's just the power trippers that seem be in control of them that worry me a little.

Because I know that lawyers want to know all the facts, it's here that I take you on the journey of 'why' it is so before we get to the 'how'.

A very long time ago, some strange things happened that you should know about because it is the very cause of your being. Those happenings resulted in you becoming the magnificent and perfect being that you are, incognito (under the Suit). You have just forgotten. Most people who think along the same lines that I do, believe that how this thing we are all involved in, called 'Life on planet Earth', started with a big bang. The Big Bang theory is a popularly endorsed scientific theory about how the universe began a whopping 13.8 billion years ago, and personally, I think what those fabulous scientists are saying seems to make sense. As famous astrophysicist, Neil deGrasse Tyson says, *"The good thing about science is that it's true whether or not you believe in it"*.

I am not going to explain the theory, because for this purpose it isn't really important. But I do want to let you know what the universe is made of. Ever wondered what it is you look at when you stare at the night sky? Yes? Good. The reliable people at NASA have discovered that only 4.6% of the entire universe is made up of atoms.[a] That, my friends, is not much at all – minuscule even! The rest has been detected as being a combination of dark energy and dark matter. It's important to understand that even those very clever scientists haven't yet really agreed on what that dark matter is, save that the dark energy appears to be responsible for the acceleration of the universe. I'll take that to mean that it has a purpose.

To break it down further, of that atomic 4.6%, only 0.00000001% of that matters (oops I mean is matter) and the remaining 99.9999999% is not. Not only do you matter, you are matter and whilst I hate to be the bearer of bad tidings, you make up rather a good deal of empty space. I'm referring here to the you that you think you are. You barely exist! There you have it.

From hero to zero, someone to no-one in approximately three seconds flat.

Sorry about that, I know you feel the empty space and, whilst it doesn't seem like it right now, I am here to help.

Now for a mini science lesson. Back in science class, if you sat toward the front, you would have been taught about atoms. If you were at the back, then you probably learned many other great life lessons. Nevertheless, a good deal has changed about the theory of atoms since I was in school, way back. However, the basics are the same. Atoms are made up of really small particles called things like electrons, neutrons and protons. Broken down even further are smaller bits called quarks, gluons (love those words) and other funny little things. Importantly, the majority of an atom is made of empty space and energy.

For instance, when an atom is split, it releases a massive amount of energy for something that barely exists. I need you to remember that energy is the important part here. I find it interesting that people have trouble grasping this science despite their ready acceptance that electricity runs through their power lines to keep their fridges running, and that there are energy waves forming pictures on their television screens for their nightly entertainment.

In a bizarre little notion scientists call quantum physics, it is shown that atoms have a rather peculiar nature. Atoms are little weirdos. They can act as waves and particles. You can't even pinpoint where one is at any given time. There is also this theory called non-locality that Albert Einstein shrugged off by calling it "*spooky actions at a distance*". Non-locality shows us that objects, even at large distances apart, can affect each other. Like, for instance, when you are thinking of someone and then they call you on the phone. Spooky indeed!

There are other really cool experiments that prove this theory, such as in the discoveries of Dr Cleve Backster. Whilst working in the area of hypnosis, Dr Backster could show that after connecting a plant to a polygraph machine (lie detector), that plants had feelings. He was also able to demonstrate, by the reaction on the polygraph machine to certain experiments he carried out, that you could shock or scare a plant![14] He took the experiment further and extracted cells from a person's mouth. With measuring devices, he revealed that there was a reaction to those cells that corresponded with that person's emotional state, even though that person was over three hundred miles away from their cells at the time.

There is a great deal more scientific evidence available verifying this phenomenon that you could check out, which even explains how teleportation could actually become a possibility. This is mind-opening information. Even science doesn't totally know why atoms can do what they do. *You* are made of this stuff. In fact, Neil deGrasse Tyson explains it better and says that we are made from the same stuff as the stars. When I heard this, I finally realised that I am a luminary. At last!

virginia
warren

LUMINARY

I think you'll all agree, it had to be done.

---

14 *This idea messed with my mind. I became a vegetarian to do my part in respect of animals. Now they tell me plants can be scared. Made me wonder whether my carrots screamed as I chopped them for dinner. Sensibly, I now speak kind words to them before I produce the knife!*

Think about it. Your heart beats by itself, you breathe while you're asleep, and that neat slice you made in your hand from chopping last night's onions will disappear all by itself. You, and all the cells and atoms that make up you, are awesome and no-one has yet categorically formulated how this awesomeness15 operates. It just does. So, if I can convince you of that argument, we're halfway there. The other half is science.

Keep in mind that scientists haven't yet worked out why the things we can actually see before us behave the way they do. But it's true that a random bunch of atoms can look just like the solid chair you're sitting on. That chair is mostly empty space. Empty space, being the majority of the universe, has an unknown constitution. So most of what we think we know, is in fact, unknown. From all that, it was easy for me to rationally think there is something greater than us out there, wherever 'there' is, operating mission control. And that anything at all in this game we affectionately call Life could be a distinct possibility, and in my mind, open for debate.

---

15 *Nevertheless, there are quite a few of us that refer to this awesomeness as consciousness. More on that later.*

CHAPTER

3

Game on!

I need to ease you all into this somehow. Gently. As I mentioned previously, my first 'wow' moment in life threw itself right at me from the book by Florence Scovel Schinn – *The Game of Life and How to Play It*. A game, huh? How interesting, I thought. So I decided to make that notion my inspiration for this chapter in explaining how I conclude the game called Life ticks.

From my observations of Life generally to date, I am pretty sure that every single one of us wants to find, and remain, in our happy place. But how can we do that when it seems the bad stuff even happens to good folks? Lawyers, most of all, see that bad stuff as a first-hand experience. We get to see Life in its full blown 'glory' at the very moment it's swirling down the toilet. We get to share in the moments of our clients' struggling as their idea of Life is falling to pieces.

Let's consider the proposition for the moment, that if there is a so-called God – in the organised religious meaning of the word (no offence intended to anyone and please substitute your own deity here) – then those bad experiences should not happen. It doesn't make sense, right? So, what if there was another school of thought on why crappy things happen? Something that we could say: well, this might answer the questions. I think I've found one theory that ticks all the boxes. It seems to make sense to me anyway.

Based on the premise that the chair you're sitting on is mostly empty space, some spiritual philosophies have suggested that this life we are living is all an illusion. That the things we think exist, actually do not. Some have even come up with the idea that we are all part of a large computer game, a matrix (a bit far-fetched, I know). But what if this were true? You're getting your 'flat' eyes on, aren't you? Just stick with me a bit longer...

To illustrate my point, I am purposefully going to oversimplify the elements tongue-in-cheek style. Imagine there is this game called 'Life' and it goes like this:

- You are player one. Sometimes you can include player two, three or more.

- The game is played on planet Earth.

- You have a whole bunch of lives in the game and for each life, you choose the mission you want to conquer and how you will play that mission out.

- Mission completed, you then progress to the next level and choose a new mission.

- Fail the level and you start over.

- To master a level, you must be able to tune in to your whole true self and not let your ego mind control you and trick you into failing the mission. The ego being your rival, your opponent.

- IMPORTANT: The goal is to outplay the mastermind ego, all whilst keeping it intact, to reach a state of inner peace, happily ever after, total bliss etc., etc., – you get the picture.

- Bonus: You have helpers outside of the game.

When you play Life you have free will. Yay! The best part is that there are no real rules whilst you are in this game. I love to say that rules are for idiots.[16] Guidelines or suggestions, perhaps. Rules, not so much. You are the one who sets all the parameters to the game before you start out. The point is, if you want to progress in the game it's all up to you. Think about it. The game is all about you. Isn't that just the best thing you've heard today?

Your goal is to outplay your own ego. Release it from holding the reins. It's your ego that stands squarely in the way of you finally reaching your happy place.

Ego.

The tough, outer exterior. The identification with a self that really doesn't exist. The master of separation. The SUIT! "*Kiss my shiny metal ass!*",[17] it says. As if to think it can be kissed. Evil Suit.

To illustrate. If you are wondering, why does 'stuff' keep happening to me? Like, why can't I save money? Where is the love of my life? Or even: Why is it that I keep having to appear before Judge [*insert name of nemesis Judge here*]? It could well be that you are facing a life mission to conquer. It's a pretty good way to face a problem head on with: "*Okay, so what do I have to conquer for my betterment here?*" with your 'mission' eyes on, rather than the attitude of "*Oh... here we go again, woe is me*". This, my dearest of friends, is the essence of the game. Simple. It's all just grist for the mill.

As I go on, I will set out details of the types of Life missions you might be facing and other juicy information about the nature of our existence, along with some useful tips to help you to master Life. In other words, I'll keep it light for now, but as I go on you

---

16 *Probably got me into a little trouble when I told my then grade 1 son that information in response to a newly-imposed 'inclusion' rule at his Primary School, which said: "you can't say, you can't play". That one's a long story.*

17 *A nod to all Futurama fans.*

might like to delve a little deeper with me into some really good insider knowledge.

Are you still with me? If so... game on!

4

Meanwhile, back at the ranch

The ranch? I'm talking about 'home', the source of all creation. Where the game of Life begins. You may remember I mentioned that the word 'home' got my lights and buzzers going when I was studying yoga for my teaching qualification. *"What and where is home?"* you might ask, as did I back then. Good question! But first, I'll talk a little more about the nature of us so-called human beings.

You may (or may not) have heard it said that *"we are spiritual beings having a human experience"*. If so, and you thought that was cool, then great! You already get the basics of what I am about to explain. If not, then that's cool too. What I mean by that statement is that at our very essence, we are all energy. I've already given you a little guided tour about atoms and their weirdo behaviour. You may want to go and re-read that part if you need to brush up on your physics.

Given that atoms make up the things that you see around you, and that atoms are for the most part just energy, it figures that all the things you can see, like the chair we looked at earlier, are just energy. Your house, the trees, the dog... the dog sometimes has too much energy. You see what I'm trying to say here? Absolutely everything is made up of nothing more than little particles of energy. As Einstein succinctly puts it:

"Everything is energy and that's all there is. Match the frequency of the reality you want and you cannot help but get that reality. It can be no other way. This is not philosophy. This is physics."

Here, he was also referring to the law of attraction principles which all rely upon the principle that everything is made of energy. Even you. But you are probably wondering where that energy is hiding after an 11-hour day. Am I right?

Recall also, the theory of non-locality where objects, made up of atoms and energy, can have an effect on each other from great distances apart. I am oversimplifying this, so please explore the topic further if it takes your fancy.

What I am trying to get you to see is that theories like non-locality show us that if we can connect with objects over great distances, and that objects are just energy then it follows we are all energetically connected in the grand universal scheme of things. Very simply put, we are all connected as energetic beings.

Further, given the spooky way energy operates (spooky, I love that word), the things you *think* you see are not what they might appear to be. There are also things you can't see that exist; for instance, infra-red, or ultra violet rays. We know they exist, but with our limited human vision we can't see these frequencies of light. In fact we can only see around 0.0035% of the entire electromagnetic spectrum. This tells me that I'm not seeing much at all. Of anything really. What's the point in that? Seems like someone's hinting that a little blind faith might be needed now and then.

I'll now take you on a little adventure into how we came to be – without getting too deep at this stage. Essentially, we are all part of the universal energy. After the Big Bang and the formation of the universe, it is said that there was a perfect intelligent consciousness[18]

---

18 *That's the 'awesomeness' I referred to earlier.*

in existence. That consciousness still exists and is everywhere.

At the start of time, this fabulous faultless consciousness – perfection in every way – decided that it wanted to have different experiences. After all, let's face it, being perfect is rather boring *yawn*. So, this consciousness divided itself up and formed individual components, which some like to call energy streams. Those streams then meandered off to the corners of wherever they felt like in the grand universe to create interesting experiences. A bunch of knowledge was gathered, the good, the bad and the ugly, so as consciousness could learn. For example: "*Okay, I know what falling over and scraping my knee feels like*" or "*I know what a broken heart feels like*". You get the idea. The goal for consciousness was to undergo every experience possible to expand itself with knowledge.

This is where we humans come in, how we got this gig. Remember that the bits of consciousness separated from the whole. This is referred to as the concept of '*separation*'. It is an important concept because the feeling of separation is the fundamental cause of human angst, fear and conflict. Separation is human suffering in a nutshell. In separating, some say these streams of consciousness formed souls, being the essence of a human. But, the soul only becomes a physical human when it shows up for work on planet Earth. This is called incarnation. The word '*incarnation*' simply means '*the act of being made flesh*'. In other words, being born as a human being. The '*work*' I mentioned is the work you do on yourself, yes, on you, for the ultimate expansion of consciousness in this game called Life.

As humans, some of us have remembered consciousness and called it names like God, Allah, Jehovah, Yahweh and the like. Some even call it the Divine, the Source, the Creator, the Big Cheese or other fun names. Much depends on whether you follow any organised religion or whether you choose a name that makes you happy.

Your call, it's all the same really. I have a secret pet name I use, which I'm not going to share yet (let's face it, you hardly know me). For the purpose of my chat with you, I'm going to refer to consciousness interchangeably as the Divine, the Creator or Divine Love, or anything else that makes me happy.

To summarise, we are all part of the universal energy of consciousness and it is part of us. We are all one and the same. We decided to 'separate' for want of a better word from Source to have a human experience. We intentionally forget that we are part of perfection; to experience humanness for ourselves and for the Creator that we are a part of.

So here I'll use my favourite analogy.

It's like being a wave on the ocean. The waves pop up and, well, wave as the individuals they are. Then once they have run their course, they ease themselves back into the ocean. The waves think they are very individual, with all their differing shapes and forms. With all their thundering and tickling. But the fact is, they are just aspects of the ocean. It's the ocean from which they rose, and it's the ocean to which they return while never ever leaving their ocean-y essence.

This is a meagre representation of the law of oneness. This is a great law. Unlike the laws we're familiar with that change with the times, the law of oneness is a fundamental law of the universe that we know and live in. Work with it and you get the low-down on what this life's all about. You are in the flow. Work against it and it's like you are that one wave who tries to smash against the rocks. You end up all separated and messy (there's one at every party); nonetheless, your essence is ocean. No matter what you do, that's who you are, just like all the other waves.

I know, I know. It's a bit tricky to grasp how we can by all accounts look like perfectly separate individuals but be integrally connected to each other and to something bigger at the same time. The best part is in understanding how we are connected to each other. That's the cutting-edge concept that will make your day job more satisfying. Understanding that whatever I do for you ultimately affects me (and vice versa) is the best news ever, to say the least. Trust me on that one.

CHAPTER

5

Love Shack Baby!

"The love shack is a little old place where we can get together..."

Who doesn't love the B-52s? So now you are wondering where I'm going with this? Okay, hang in there, I will get to the point soon enough. You may or may not, however, be quite relieved to know that it's enough of the science lessons for now. This is the part where you are really going to have to have an open mind. So, brace yourself, the 'woo woo' crazy talk is headed your way.

Up until now, we have considered how we are all primarily energy and that energy is the core of our very being. Now you probably want to know some more about the how's and why's of us happening to be these so called '*spiritual beings in human bodies*'. Or indeed, who we are when we are at 'home', and not hanging out as being human.

There is not much science to explain what the story really is, only the say so of some people, that, well, say so. Happily, there is some nearly tangible evidence available explaining our real nature, shared by people that have had what is called a Near Death Experience (loving a good acronym as I do, they will hereinafter be referred to as 'NDEs').

These people, and there are thousands and thousands of them, have reported on the super cool things that happened to them during their time in a deep coma, or even after having been declared clinically dead.

One notable person having reported on such an experience was Dr Eben Alexander, a respected neurosurgeon who, back in 2008 remained in a coma from meningitis for seven days. Another is Anita Moorjani, a cancer patient who was declared clinically dead and, in her words, "returned to her body" by choice (that's an important aspect). In Anita's case, her body was riddled with cancer at the time of her death, but just days after her return to life, her cancer was gone! I urge you to look up each of their stories, you will be amazed. There are also websites where thousands of people share similar stories. There is much to learn from NDEs, so I will conveniently use their general themes now and then to illustrate the various curious aspects of our true nature.

After studying oodles of those experiences, I would like to highlight two notable characteristics common to the majority. The most important is that we don't actually die in the manner most people believe. What appears to happen is that we return to our energetic state. Some people fondly refer to this as 'spirit', and as I have likened it previously, to going 'home'. We just shed our human form and leave it behind. Our energetic, or spirit self, which is also commonly referred to (for the sake of convenience in this context) as our soul, is now free. Free from the drama. Free from the heaviness of it all. Home free. Woo hoo!

And yes, importantly, despite what people have said about lawyers, we fit into the category of human complete with soul. The real you, the energetic you, remains unaffected, save that you are pretty damn happy to be rid of that old dead weight, pardon the pun. You are now in a space where the oneness law is apparent to you. After hanging out for a bit, you then might choose to go on to play another level in the game.

The second, and the most fabulous point in my humble opinion, is that it's the *'Love Shack'* where we go when we die. Sorry, I had to say that. I am calling it the Love Shack because I like the sound of it and because it's a pretty good description of the state of affairs you find yourself in, based on what I've read. From all accounts, it would appear that love is the main ingredient of the going-home experience.

Whilst those NDE'ers report on other amazing things they have encountered, it is love that is the common thread that ties the vast majority of reported experiences together. It is the 'be all and end all' of everything. It seems that you return to a place where love is all that matters. Love is all there is. It forms a fundamental component of the energy making up the universe and who we all are at the core of our very being.

This may help comfort you if you have had the unfortunate experience of losing someone close, and it is one of the most important snippets of information I need you to take away from this. I'll say it again. *Love is all that matters, and it is part of the energy making up who we are.* It *is* who we are. We are love. I will even go as far to say that some of the NDE'ers report that when they return to their bodies, they are as mad as hell about it, 'cause they've *'lost that lovin' feeling...'*.

The unconditional love they experienced is beyond the comprehension of us mere mortals. Just as well, otherwise we wouldn't continue with the challenges this nasty old game has on offer. I will talk further about the nature of these challenges as we progress.

As I mentioned earlier, scientifically speaking, much of the energy in the universe has not been conclusively identified. At one stage, there was a letter circulating that Einstein supposedly wrote to his daughter Lieserl. The letter was later discovered not to be written by Einstein at all; however, the words are so beautiful, and speak the words of so many others, that I'm inspired to share an extract:

> *"When scientists looked for a unified theory of the universe they forgot the most powerful unseen force. Love is Light, that enlightens those who give and receive it. ... This force explains everything and gives meaning to life. This is the variable that we have ignored for too long, maybe because we are afraid of love because it is the only energy in the universe that man has not learned to drive at will."*

Despite the lack of scientific evidence to date, it remains a theory that love is quite probably that mysterious energy that can't be explained. The stuff that fills up the empty space. I know we do *feel* emptiness without it. Nonetheless, it is what we are surrounded, blanketed and immersed in when we leave our human form behind and return to our natural energetic state ... *'cause love rules, at the love shack.*

CHAPTER

6

Love is a four-letter word

At least that's what some of my family law clients say. I have previously had a chat to you about the idea of love. Not just any kind of love, not the romantic stuff that makes retailers money. Think Valentine's day. Not the erotic business (I didn't think I'd go there) and not the heart-breaking kind my clients are referring to. I'm referring to the type of love I touched upon in the previous chapter, quite possibly the very fabric of the universe, the blank in the universal equation, the filling of the 99.9999999% of unidentified space, the most phenomenally, out of this world unconditional type of love you can't even imagine. So how do I explain?

I challenge anyone to even describe what love from a human perspective feels like. We could start with warm, fuzzy, gooey or [*insert other similar adjectives here*] type of love. Hmmm??? Love, from our point of view is admittedly rather hard to describe. It isn't too hard to guess then, that a description of the real deal, that universal love I was referring to, eludes me completely as I have no personal frame of reference to rely upon. So, as promised, I return to the reliance I have upon those trusty peeps having had NDEs to guide the way on this one, for they claim that they have encountered this love first-hand.

From the more renowned experiences such as that of Anita Moorjani, who recalls: *"... I actually 'crossed over' to another dimension, where I was engulfed in a total feeling of love. The amount of love I felt was overwhelming..."*. To others of the many thousands I have read about, who commonly describe the love they felt in words like: *"pure and total"*, *"absolutely outrageously incredible"* and *"unconditional"*.

To illustrate further, I have chosen to quote these beautiful words which nicely sum up the experience of NDE'er Nancy Rynes:

> *"...the sense [of] love completely ensnared me and made me want to stay there forever. I felt a deep sense of that love flowing through all things around me... I felt the love flowing around me, flowing through me, and eventually capturing me by the heart. I felt supported by a loving Presence so powerful, yet so gentle, that I cried again. I had never experienced such unconditional love and acceptance in all of my years on the planet. It felt as though this place were built from love and peace on a very grand, cosmic scale."*

Breath-taking description. *Sigh!* Who wouldn't LOVE that?!

Understandably, and as I briefly mentioned previously, there are some NDE'ers who, after having found themselves soaking in the all-encompassing splendour of this love, are somewhat put out by having to return to their mission, to the front line, the coalface. Back squarely in the centre of this game called Life. I imagine you can gather by now, love of this magnitude and magnificence is well beyond the comprehension of us humble humans. But of course, there is a reason for that. You are not meant to want to go home whilst on a Life mission. It defeats the purpose.

You are supposed to have forgotten your true nature so that you don't get homesick, so you don't want to go back before you're done. No "beam me up, Scotty" to be had here.[19]

The very existence of this type of love goes hand-in-hand with the concept of non-judgement. You are unconditionally loved at your very core. Yes, loved, without any conditions whatsoever being attached. It follows then that you are not judged for the job you do here, contrary to the general view of organised religions and the court process. Two fine institutions right there. In fact, after your mission is complete, when you return home, you get to check out the stats. How did you go on planet Earth? Did you in fact conquer your mission? Did you go out in a blaze of glory for handling your mission in the best possible way? Or, did you just go off the rails completely ... bah-bow! Do not pass Go, do not collect $200! In the latter case, it doesn't matter. You are not judged, just guided as to better options so you can have another shot at it.

Whilst on Earth, we are designed to live under what some fondly refer to as, 'the veil of forgetfulness'. I remind people of that often, as I justify my quest for the missing car keys. It seems we have agreed to forget that we really are these perfectly divine loving beings, so that we can complete our missions.

The simplest of theories seems to go something like this: if you knew everything was going to turn out just fine, that you couldn't make any mistakes, then you wouldn't challenge yourself. The funny part, one you will often find me in the corner laughing to myself about is, that when you remember who you really are then you enjoy the challenges. You understand that they are all about your evolution. It's a paradox really. That's why I want as many people as I can to hear the message that they are pure love. And that they are here to remember that about themselves and evolve. It gives the conflicts in your life purpose and value.

---

19 *Apologies to the non-Star Trek fans – oh and I won't mention the whole Trekkies vs Trekkers debate, it's simply not in the loving spirit of this discussion.*

The position is then, that the ultimate exam on Earth University comprises how you go at experiencing this human life to the fullest, without first remembering that we are love incarnate. One vital component of life experience is found in our feelings. You have to feel this world. All of it.

Within your experiencing comes your innate creative abilities. Don't worry if you can't draw or sing. I'll sing for you. There are many ways to be creative. You can even be a creator as a lawyer. For instance, you might want to create a better way of practising law. Let me know. We'll be best friends.

My personal goals and friendship circles aside, in addition to experiencing this life and creating wonderful things, the objective is to bring out our characteristic trait – unconditional love. First and foremost, we must do this for ourselves. It's only then that we can deliver it to others on planet Earth, all whilst living in a relatively hostile environment. It's the *'put your own mask on before helping others'*, type of scenario.

Loving ourselves? Wow. That's a tough one. We do this by conquering that fear-mongering ego we have carefully nurtured at the guidance of our well-meaning parents and cultivated further through law school. No easy task, that sucker is doing a job on each and every one of us! We've built our ego into such an impenetrable monster that the real, totally lovable you, has remained hog-tied. So the real four-letter word should stand for: Living Outside the Veil of Ego. Tough mission, thanks a bunch, mission control! AND just when you thought that might be an easy ride, along the way we also have our personal missions to deal with, to enhance our own evolution.

I will explain later a little about the types of missions you might have asked to accomplish and how you asked for this mission all by yourself. Yes, ASKED for them. You're clever. And a super hero. Hero also has four letters. You are Helping Everyone Realise Ourselves. Not great grammar, but a fun acronym! I'll show you how to do this later, the helping, that is, not so much the grammar.

CHAPTER

7

I see you're back in town?

I walked you through the idea that most of us cannot understand why bad things happen to good people. In fact, it is usually the reason people exclaim: "*There is no God!*" Fair enough. But what if I could give you a plausible reason as to why those nasty things happen? You do want to know. It will enhance the reasons why you do your day job. Well you will need to take a seat, and a nice deep breath.

Drum roll please!

You planned for those things to happen. All of it, the good, the bad and the ugly!! Yep, you even planned for your stepmother to whack you with a wooden spoon for the things your sister did! Well, not in that much detail, but you did plan to have your evil stepmother [*or replace with other crazed human*] in your life. It's all about the particular mission you wished to conquer in this game called Life.

I know, in the last chapter I promised I would talk about how brave you are in making and planning those missions. Especially if it involved an evil step-mother, but I do need to back up a bit. I'm getting way ahead of myself. Love a good mission as I do, I need you to know a little about a neat process called reincarnation before we go much further.

Remember when I described incarnation as meaning 'in the flesh'? Well, literally 're'-incarnation means going back in the flesh. Right now, I'm seeing flinches and hearing sounds of "ew!". You love it actually, as it allows you to swing by planet Earth every now and then to have a shot at your latest endeavour. The reason you do it is to better your good self, and in turn better the rest of us. There's that oneness factor again.

Evidence that reincarnation may be a reality has come to our attention via our good friends the hypnotherapists. People have been taken on journeys via hypnotherapy to check out who they were in past lives. There, they often discover things that happened to them which is presently causing them some grief in this lifetime. For instance, you may be suffering from a pain in your back that no-one can resolve. You have some hypnotherapy and are taken to a past life showing that you were in the French Foreign Legion in the late 1800s and were poked really hard in the back by your buddy's out of control bayonet. There is evidence that remembering past events like these have in fact cured people's ailments. This gives us some indication that there just might be something really cool in exploring the notion of past lives being a reality.

You're doing it now, aren't you? You are having a little think about the journeys you personally might have been on. Do you have an unexplained affinity for a food, place or culture? It may just be an imprint of a past life that you wanted to remain with you on this round.

To recap then. If you have reincarnated, it follows you have probably lived before. After your time is done being in a physical body, you return to spirit to regroup, take a rest. It's rough going on Earth... *nah, you don't say*? You then have a natter about your last mission, have a bit of a gossip about who's doing what lately, and then make grand plans for your next life. Then off you go again.

It should figure that your mode of transportation to the next mission is via childbirth and, you won't understand this right now, but... wait for it... you choose your parents! Yes, read it again. You. Choose. Your. Parents! For some of you that's a horrifying thought and you are wondering what the hell is wrong with you. Trust me, it's all good, but I'll get to that more fully later.

The interesting thing is that after we are born, we are still very connected to home. We are born as perfection itself. We expect that love will be given to us unconditionally, because that's who we are. We remain that way for a few years until we are conditioned to obeying the parenting-styles dished up by the well-meaning (or otherwise) adults or authority figures in our young lives. We rely on those adults for our survival, so we dutifully do (or don't do) certain things to secure their acceptance. Seeking that acceptance can make us or break us. I discuss how this happens in Part III.

This strong connection to our energetic selves whilst we're very young has come to light in cases where very young children – of around two or three years of age – spontaneously start talking about something completely bizarre, like: "*My other mummy has curly hair*", or "*I like my other house better*" and other weird things which are completely inexplicable to their stunned parents. Naturally, those parents think their babies are playing make believe. But in cases where the '*game*' the child is playing becomes persistent, and where the child is referring to adult matters they could not possibly know about, or even understand given their age, parents have taken the next step and examined the issue further.

In these instances, parents have investigated what their child has said and have connected the facts to those of a person having passed away. It could be a relative or a stranger. All information gathered then points to the distinct probability of the child being a reincarnation of said passed-away person. These young children, for some reason, appear to remember more clearly their connection to the other realms. It is not an unusual phenomenon and is widely reported. For instance, Carol Bowman published a book called *Children's Past lives* in 1997, which discusses many astounding case studies. It's worth a read if you're interested.

Though there are many, there is one extraordinary story I need to tell you about. James Leininger was at the time a two year old, appearing on all fronts to be a regular little boy who spent his time engrossed in playing with his toy planes. His parents began to become concerned when he would more frequently wake in the night screaming in terror: *"Plane on fire! Little man can't get out."* Scary stuff for parents. You parents with toddlers will understand that one. The toddler is there screaming, but literally there appears to be no-one home.

Subsequent to James explaining complex and unusual parts of a war plane, his mother Andrea speculated that perhaps he was a World War II fighter pilot in a former life. She mentioned this to her husband Bruce, who, being a God-fearing man, thought her suggestion was a lot of nonsense. One day his sceptical father asked James who the *'little man'* was. James told his father matter-of-factly that the *'little man'* was him, and then made a disgusted face whilst telling his father that his plane was shot down by the Japanese. His father wasn't at all convinced by this, and upon further questioning, James told his father that he was flying a Corsair plane that was launched from a boat called the *Natoma*.

Undertaking some serious research, his father was surprised to learn that the *Natoma Bay* was in fact a World War II aircraft carrier and James even correctly identified the place on a map where his plane was shot down. After further extensive verification (including discussion with surviving war veterans who could validate the information), Bruce accepted the likelihood that little James was in fact James Huston Jnr whose plane was shot in the engine and caught fire, exactly as described by two-year-old James. I need to mention here that Bruce struggled greatly with reconciling this discovery against his strong religious background. This story has many awesome facts that, by all accounts, appear not be co-incidental. Please do look this up, you'll get tingles (love tingles).

These stories also suggest that in certain cases, past lives can have an impact on this lifetime. It is also some validation for the idea that young children remain connected to the other realm up until about age four or five, or until we older spoilsports ruin it for them and make them live in our acceptance-seeking reality. So, we need to urge parents, teachers and guardians to pay attention to the small children in their charge when they say interesting things.

Enough about that, we need to get on with knowing what we're doing here in the first place.

CHAPTER

8

Your mission,
should you choose to accept it

What prompts you intelligent beings to leave bliss behind, go back through the veil of forgetfulness, just to revisit this hell on Earth? ... And become a lawyer?

To play the game of course!

You love this game. You get to conquer your missions and move through the levels. In this, and the next chapter, I will explain a little about the background behind choosing these missions and all about you getting yourself especially frocked up for your short outings to Earth. I should remind you right here, that one lifetime is mighty short in the scheme of things. Then later, I will delve into the how's and why's of your choices to get down and dirty as you roll your sleeves up to start work here on this planet. Yes, you do start out all shiny but it all thunders downhill from there. Temporarily. And for good reason.

I'll just take a little step to the right before I get going. I need you to understand that one of the best parts about your trips back to humanity is that you usually incarnate with a bunch of your besties and these peeps are called your soul group. These are the ones who frequently show up as members of your current family and circle of friends. There may also be a cameo here and there from others when you least expect it. And, just to make it clear, you probably won't recognise these guys at all. So, when your superior is sending you out to get the coffees for the third time this week, or when you're again trying to reason with nasty Mrs Jones who wants to cut her doting husband out of her will again, these 'lovely' people are helping you. They love you deeply and have agreed to join you in your quest. You are now thinking about certain people that fit those descriptions and are scratching your head with a look of: '*No way!*' Well, just hang in there, it all comes together a bit further down the track.

Speaking of parents, remember I said that you *chose* them? Whilst there are many recounted stories on this topic, I'll take you back to the last chapter where I referred to little James Leininger, whom his shocked parents discovered was the reincarnation of World War II fighter pilot James Huston Jnr. Imagine his parents' disbelief when James also told his father: *"I knew you would be a good daddy, that's why I picked you"*, and that he'd found them *"In Hawaii, at the pink hotel, on the beach"*. His father no doubt felt faint as James described his parents' fifth wedding anniversary in detail, being five weeks before his wife fell pregnant. Awesome.

Well, what are these missions and why do we have them?

First, our missions are the things we want to achieve here on planet Earth that, once successfully completed, allow us to proceed to the next level. Now, I have again over-simplified that thing about 'levels' just for gaming-type illustration purposes. And for the purpose of staying in tune with the old KISS rule.[20] There are no such things as 'levels'.

Remember how I have explained to you we are all one? We are just

---

20 *You know I love a good kiss, but not so much a good rule. Let's call it the KISS suggestion: Keep It Simple Stupid.*

different aspects of the one. This means I cannot be better, grander, or a snappier dresser than you, and you cannot look down on me because I have only completed two missions and you are up to your tenth mission (and own two Armani suits). The idea is, succeeding in life's missions helps us to raise our energetic vibration so that we get closer to a wonderful state known as ultimate bliss. That's our inner peace maxed out. I guess I could explain it in terms of lightness.

For example, remember when you snuck out early Christmas morning and saw that shiny new pushbike under the tree? Well you thought all your Christmases had come at once, didn't you? You were bursting with so much happiness that you thought you would explode, and you literally felt all light and floaty as you bounced quietly back to bed. That's the kind of lightness I'm talking about. This is to be totally contrasted with the feeling you had when you found out that the bike was for your little brother! You felt 'down in the dumps', that heavy, sinking feeling, where bed looked like the best place to be for the rest of your life. This 'lightness index' works on a scale something like that, the more missions you succeed in, the lighter and more "woo-hoo!" you become. You don't just feel it, you *become* it. The good news is, you can bring this feeling of lightness into your everyday life.

Now to expand further on the lightness and ultimate bliss thing, let's go back to where I talked about how consciousness, in its unquestionable perfection, wanted to get out of the house and start to live a little. To explain, I am going to get you to put your director's hat on to create a clichéd little film in your head...

"*Action!*"

Open to image of fairy-tale princess cooped up in paradise. There she is, resplendent to be seen, sitting on her gold-braided, purple silk cushion, filing her nails whilst her servants bring her tea and chocolate cookies on a silver platter. Yes, the cookies needed to be chocolate and I probably should have added that the silver platter is diamond encrusted.

Anyway, the central theme is this: Princess yawns and complains about her boring life whilst examining her perfect manicure. She breaks free from constraints of castle to see how other half lives using well-orchestrated plan, usually with pet. Said pet representing the mature voice of reason. Princess meets bad boy and has some wild ego-centric experiences. Princess learns some valuable life-changing lessons appreciating how other half lives, all the while balking at now damaged manicure (I hate it when that happens!). Bad boy realises his true nature and becomes good boy. Good boy gets to live with Princess in paradise. Everyone, along with now miffed pet, gets to live happily ever after. Standard formula.

That, my friends, is a parallel of your trip. Your essence, your soul, is an impeccably flawless piece of the mighty perfection that is called consciousness. The perfection that is you accumulates certain rather emotionally-taxing and unpleasant experiences. Said unpleasant experiences generally happen in early childhood and are carried around with you as your little burden to bear. You need to see how the other half lives. How humans live as 'conditionally' loved. As opposed to that beautiful unconditional love you are used to experiencing. You design these interesting life experiences to challenge yourself to see if you can remember who you are. You are on a quest to realise your true nature and experience the paradise of eternal bliss all while living through hell.

The more levels you master, the more you can experience and complete the various aspects of your true self and the greater your bragging rights become. You can then say to the 'newer' souls, *"Yeah, been there done that... it was rough going but, you know, it was worth it"*. You should see it when those newer souls just stand there and gape in awe of your added sparkle.

Following on, I'll now touch on the concept of why bad things happen to good people. I hear cries all the time of: "*If there were a God, how could He let this happen!*". Aside from the point I've made previously that, in my view, such a finger pointing, all-smiting individual does not exist as such. The boss of the universe is consciousness itself, and as you are a small piece of that consciousness, then it is you.

You are the boss. Yay, great news! Oh, hang on, so am I...

For each lifetime that you choose to pop back onto this noble blue planet, you, as the fine boss of you that you are, will have previously set one or more fun lessons for yourself to learn. These lessons, or challenges, will occur all whilst trying to reign in that nasty little number called the human ego in the process. Tough gig.

For instance, you may want to learn to overcome assertiveness. An oversimplified example of a way to master that issue is, you choose the parents that are going to be verbally abusive to you, so you think that the only way to get love from them is to be 'good' and act as a door mat. You now successfully carry the 'vibe' of timidity as your subconscious signature. You will then attract a partner that will serve up your signature dish in an abusive marriage.

Your timidity will be staring you right in the face each time you are abused. No laughing matter. To overcome your timidity, you have to outwit your ego as it will keep telling you that you are a door mat and that is all you will ever be. In this case, ego's nature will fight you tooth and nail to bring you right back down into your door mat status every time. This is where the challenge comes in. It's you – versus you. You versus your own ego in the quest to find your way back to wholeness. There are two of you in there, you know. Picture the cartoon with an angel on one shoulder and devil on the other. It's a little like that. Anyway, and importantly, it's not you versus your abuser, nor is it you versus the rest of humanity.

Yes, you may have to defend yourself from time to time, but attacking anyone, including your good self, is not on. Ego is a major player in life's quandaries. I will offer up some strategies for you to lovingly reign in that intruder in your head as we progress.

In the example I've provided on learning to be assertive, once you have cleared your self-limiting beliefs that you are no more than a victim; once you can assert yourself, you have reclaimed that aspect of yourself and that particular challenge you set for this lifetime resolves. You win! For *yourself*. Mission accomplished. If you don't learn from the challenge it will be back to visit you over and over via different abusers until you finally lick it.

Please know that I am very serious when I say, it's not okay to be abused. Abuse is immoral and, in most cases, as we know, illegal. The abuser may nevertheless remain in your life for other reasons and you should seek help. Getting help from others is part of the game also – it could be part of the another person's mission to rescue those who are abused. What I am saying is often there is deeper meaning to why a person might remain in the situation.

It could likely be the abuser is also trying to learn something, like defeating their own subconscious when it rises to challenge them in their low self-esteem department. From what I have learned to date, this whole issue is highly complex, and I am only touching briefly upon it to give you a heads up if you wish to explore the matter further. There is complex planning in the preparation of each of your missions. And rest assured, you do head bravely out into the wilderness with solid backup.

Recall I talked about your soul group, well they all have to agree on the role they are to play. So, in the first example I provided on the assertiveness lesson, you would have pre-planned when and where you were going to meet up with your spouse. This is a very intricate topic and one you really need to get your head around. To better understand why and how we choose these challenges, along with examples of the lessons you might want to have learned, I can refer you to Robert Schwartz's book, *Your Soul's Plan*. It really does need a whole book to give you better insight.

Also, I should let you know that your soul group often consists of people you have reincarnated with many times around. Some of those 'delights', especially the most difficult ones, are there as a major part of your mission. You can think to yourself, *"Hi in there, Aunt Rosie, I remember you from lifetime number 576 and that whole cheesecake incident."* Those annoying people in your life are facing you smack bang, head on, with a lesson you have set for yourself. You planned it all. You definitely now have my permission to roll your eyes at that one! Okay, and then take a big sigh. Acceptance is really a good thing at this point.

CHAPTER

9

It's karma, Jim, but not as we know it...

Let's travel back to where I explained that the missions you plan to carry out on Earth are designed to help you learn lessons, and to experience all there is out there to experience. It is important to say here that some encounters here on Earth are had for the purpose of balancing out some karma, which is also all wrapped up in a mission.

For instance, you may wonder why your mother is treating your naughty siblings like angels but when it comes to you, you and your 'A' grades at school were never good enough. In this instance, it's quite possible you're on the receiving end of some karmic debt you promised to balance out. You may have been her big brother in a previous life and always beat her up. You would have both agreed in this lifetime, that her being emotionally unavailable to you is the best way of you experiencing her 'beating you up', figuratively speaking. You may have planned this state of affairs so it became part of the 'be assertive' mission you're on. Karma is not payback in the nasty sense. Remember, we come from a place of love, it's just that this way you both get to understand each side of the one experience.

To recap, karma is not punishment for being rotten. Remember, there is no such thing as punishment. Karma is simply played out as a soul experience. What better way for souls to experience both sides of the one coin than two souls being opposing actors in their respective scenarios. Now have a bit of a think about the relationships you are in presently and consider what your missions could be and/or what karma is being played out. This is the coolest part. Life here on planet Earth is all about relationships. A difficult situation stoushed in conflict can take on an entirely new meaning when you look at it like that. You know, once you've learned a lesson, more often than not the designated perpetrator no longer serves a purpose and magically disappears from your life. I've had first-hand experience with that magic. If they don't disappear, your perception of them shifts and in effect the person they were, to you, is no longer an issue.

I want to make a further big distinction. Your missions aren't your life's purpose. During this lifetime, you also try to live your purpose whilst carrying out the missions and balancing some karma along the way. Living your purpose means doing that thing that makes your essence, the core of your very being, your soul, happy, contented and all warm and fuzzy. And importantly, it means *not* listening to that psycho of an ego of yours which is telling you that your purpose is to rule the world, enslaving all creatures great and small that attempt to thwart your goal!

Do. Not. Listen. It's a dirty little trickster. It likes to keep you in a state of separation for its own preservation purposes. It loves us to forget our true nature.

Our life's purpose is different for all of us, but it is most certainly based somewhere in creativity, experiences and service to others. And when I say 'service' to others, the service comes from your choice to serve. For instance, you decide you want to spend your life working as a chocolatier. Yum! You love creating arty chocolates and your service to others comes from the delicious creations you sell. That's the kind of service I am talking about. The kind that shares your fine talents.

You are a born creator, a natural observation seeing that you are just a mere slice of the all-knowing perfection that is consciousness. It is our job to create, experience and serve. Being true to your purpose makes you feel light as a feather and you just *know* that you are on the money. You feel full up inside; complete even. You might get this feeling when you're crocheting a warm scarf for your mum, or even when you're mowing the lawn. *Mowing the lawn?* Yes, some people are even fulfilling their purpose in obtaining great satisfaction from cultivating a luscious lawn without a blade of grass out of place. It is all about creating something others will appreciate.

Importantly, you know that you are not living your purpose when you feel plain miserable. You feel it. Right in your heart. It's a heavy feeling. Sadly, a symptom of this can sometimes manifest in addictions. You are trying to fill the space with a temporary bit of pleasure that your true purpose should be fulfilling. What I do need you to know right now is that you can actually be living true to your purpose whilst tackling some tricky missions all the while balancing out some karma.

Just keep karma and carry on.

CHAPTER

10

Mission complete, what next?

What then happens after you've completed your life's work? Well usually, as word in the other realm has it, you are greeted by predeceased family members, or even by close friends, some that you would not even have known whilst here on Earth, to settle you back in. Once you're all settled, your helpers take charge and ask you to take a deep breath and sit down so you can commence your evaluation. Who are these so-called helpers, you may rightly ask? They are beings, but not human beings. Again, this information is primarily obtained from evidence provided from NDE'ers and others having been clinically regressed by hypnotherapy. You may call it fiction, but it's an engaging story nonetheless. Perhaps I could make a movie?

In between our lives on Earth, you may recall that we regroup and discuss our triumphs and our fiascos to see how we can do better on the next round. This is where we have the bonus of our 'life lines', our helpers, to objectively check us out and give us a little nudge to better our chances of success next time. These helpers include beings referred to as our guides along with other wonderful etheric beings of energy you might have heard referred to as angels. They can and do help us whilst we're here on Earth, but only if we ask. It is very important that you remember that one of the main rules of the game of Life is that you have free will fulfilling your missions on Earth. Your helpers *cannot* interfere unless you ask.

Many people can make biblical references on this point. One fine example of this is, "*Ask, and it will be given to you.*" Matthew 7:7. Remember, I am not at all religious, and it's quite okay if you think it's too much to accept that other unseen entities can help us with our day-to-day lives. Yet thinking that I am alone, with no guidance on how I came to be here and what I am supposed to be doing with my life, could not be scarier, so I choose to believe those helpers are there. I call on them all they time, they are with me and are the cheer squad for 'Team Virginia'. I laugh as I write this, knowing I need them more than ever on this endeavour!

Back to the evaluation on how you did. It's said that your life literally flashes before your eyes. Again, this is a near death experience reference. You might recall that people often say when they are frightened out of their wits, or close to death, that their life flashed before their eyes. Well, apparently, this is the case. Some even say it looks like a film of their life playing before them. You are the actor in this film and you are the only audience member. You are the one that will sit there and grimace as you watch yourself stealing Mrs Dibbs's prize-winning rose from her garden. You really feel all these experiences, embarrassment, elation and all. The important thing here is that there is no judgement.

This, my friends, is despite being told from those of religious origins that you'll be banished to hell for doing naughty things. Here, in fact, all that happens is that you have to relive those unpleasant experiences and feel them for yourself. In the other realm, a red face and grimace from your good self is enough to get the idea that your behaviour was based in fear and not love. Remember when we go home, love is all there is. If you take a look at all your past actions from a place of love, there are no doubt going to be some cringe-worthy things you did that you're not proud of.

Remember, you will not burn in hell. There is only love, people! I cannot emphasise that enough. You, being the loving being you truly are, know the error of your ways and you know what you should have done in each situation. Your levels of naughtiness will therefore just probably be factored in to your next mission, or the one after that, so you can learn to appreciate someone else's prize-winning rose from afar.

Now, if you're really horrid, really rotten, and I don't need to draw you a diagram of what types of deeds you would need to have done to get yourself into this category, you are subjected to rigorous tutorials on how to play nicer before you're allowed to play the game again, before you can progress further.

Playing the game is a privilege.

I will digress here, partly because you know how I like a good digression and partly to remind you that the reason you want to play the game is to gather life experiences, to rein in the scheming ego for your completeness. In doing so you raise your vibration toward reaching your happy place, eternal bliss, nirvana. If you were at all wondering, you can raise your vibration by not taking any missions. You can, in fact, kick back at home. But according to all sources this takes a very, very, very, long time to achieve your goal. Mind you, as life is eternal, I guess that you want to experience that happy place as soon as you can. The point is, that playing the game of Life isn't a right, it's a privilege. You're elevating yourself higher on the bliss scale every time you've successfully completed a mission.

It takes a very strong soul to come to Earth. To forget all the good stuff that you left behind to deal with the rough stuff you're about to face. It is important, therefore, to view everyone dealing with some sort of trauma, or some major issue, as a person who is seeking to better themselves. Your help in their mission helps them, it also helps you. This is especially great news as a lawyer. So, if you see someone suffering, help them where you can. Remember we are part of the one. If I help you, it helps me in the end. Help your opponent. What affects you affects me, too. Be of service. See the suffering for what it is. You never know, you may have pre-planned for a particular person to come into your life to see if your good service skills are up to scratch. And next time you see the Girl Guides coming down the driveway to sell cookies, don't release the hounds. Buy a packet and take them over to old Mrs Dibbs (payback for the rose incident).

Now do you see what it's all about?

You are perfection itself, gathering experiences. You came to this planet with a plan, which in this lifetime, or for some of it at least, just happened to be lawyering. You wanted to help people, heal them, nurture and guide them. Given the unusual nature of your chosen profession, you faced a great deal of inherent conflict, angst and fear. You ended up a little lost on the way, and left wondering what this was all about.

You are now aware that you need to take care of you. That is your priority. There's that *'stick the old oxygen mask on yourself first'* metaphor again. The missing *peace* you have been looking for is centred in love, it resides in your heart. It's the trifecta in the peace diagram. It is part of you and it needs to be taken out for a walk. You are eternally an energetic being, but whilst you're doing your bit on this planet you are three neat parts. Body, mind and heart. You must nurture them equally to feel whole, at the same time keeping the ego part of the mind gently subdued.

You need to take care of all these components to feel whole and to bask in the innate peace you are seeking. You now understand that you have a real purpose, and that the relationships with your colleagues, clients and family are all part of this game. Those relationships are external. To help you understand those external relationships we need to balance our internal one first.

You are now unveiled, unmasked. Your essence is stripped naked from the clutches of the Evil Suit of separation, the ego, and you are present for all the world to see in your true kissable glory. You are the stuff the stars are made of, you are magnificent, and you didn't have to even try. You are more powerful that you realise, and you are love itself. Now you can use your superpowers for good instead of evil. For oneness rather than separateness.

If you approach the game remembering who you are, coming from that beautiful place of love, and in turn reminding yourself that we are all one, then your mission will be a grand success. You will relegate that Suit to the back of the closet so it can share in your special occasions when it behaves. In the words of the inspirational Bo Lozoff: "*We're all doing time*" here on planet Earth. It's how you do it that matters. How you find space for your heart, body and mind to speak with love in every scenario. You got this! I'm counting on you.

In the next part, I'm going to show you how it's done.

PART III

The operative part

CHAPTER

1

Point me to the rocky road

So, where were we?

Oh yes. If you were one of those people who skipped over the secret sealed business, I see you like to cut to the chase. I like your style. I, too, like to know the end first, but trust me when I tell you it's the plot that makes things exciting. Let's face it, if we just skipped to happily ever after, there would be no nail-biting suspense. You would also miss all the ingredients crucial to your way in to formulating that blissful state of 'you are now certifiably kissable'.[21]

In the first part of this book, I left you with a chilling realisation. That being, we lawyers are missing a vital element in making us the whole kissable package. In the second part, I took a side step and presented you with some hypotheses as to why we even exist at all. From my way of thinking, if you understand why you're here, the 'what you need to do to make it all worthwhile', takes better care of itself. In Part II, I also gave you the heads up as to what we've been missing – a connection with our hearts. In this Operative Part III, I will guide you down the road to finding that elusive connection and when we've navigated all the twists and turns, you will be wondering where you've been all your life.

---

21 *Yes, you do get a certificate. Or certified. One or the other, I can't remember which.*

Before we start on our travels, I'm going to stir things up a little more.

Fun, aren't I?

This is where I get you acquainted with the idea that you need to understand that being the exact opposite of happy is essential to absorbing what happy really means. I know, I know. That's not what you wanted to hear. At first I get you all excited by my overt flaunting of the word heart and the way to connect with it all, like we've opened a treasure chest, and then I cruelly go and shut the lid with the idea that this inner peace business starts from a place of being the exact opposite of happy. Sorry to burst the proverbial bubble, but that's the issue in a nutshell. I will also show you how that unhappy place is indeed where you find the treasure.

There really is a happily ever after, however the skills lie in clearing the path to it.

To explain my meaning, the great majority of us keep running from the paradoxical opportunities staring us right in the face. We're missing the vital sign posts. Chopping them down even. The fortunate ones among us get to understand there is real meaning in the journey to your happy place. So yes, you really should sit through the whole movie. The ups and the downs, the bumps in the road. And, no, you really shouldn't cover your eyes at the scary parts. You need to experience those too.

Trust me, to save you from pain, I did initially try formulating my prescription for that elusive inner peace by pondering the important question: *'would having that heroic [insert prince or princess] rescue us with a magical kiss, make us more kissable?'* Surely like attracts like. If so, would it release us from the spell cast upon us by the general public that we are really toads in disguise?

Whilst a kiss from a favourite person is without doubt something that can make our day, it doesn't change us at a fundamental level. Either the kiss is not magical, or we are not toads. Recall my sage advice that external things, whilst delivering up some internal, albeit temporary magical moments of happiness, is not where it's at. It's not the key to 'happily ever after'. It's more like 'happy just for now'. And, at the core of our being, we are not toads, so a kiss from royalty is not going to indelibly assist us.

Let's step back in time to once again review how we developed this safe and sturdy armour-plating of ours. Back to how we became so hard-wired at the 'crush, kill, destroy', win at all costs, zero-sum game methodology.

In law school, analytical skills, strategic thinking, reasoning, logic, and ticking all sorts of boxes form the set of necessary tools we are trained to use to complete the lawyer's intelligence kit. We will screw, hammer and tighten those words, sculpting them until they resemble something like the picture of truth we are building for our client. Credit where credit's due, it is creativity at its finest.[22] Despite us not being trained in creativity, you can clearly see it's a skill lawyers do possess. Nevertheless, it's the result of the training we've endured, to deploy our skillset within this entrenched institutionalised system, that's led us to a rote way of thinking. We call it our legal mind. And according to we lawyers, that's a real thing.

That legal mind has been trained to think of all contingencies, all permutations and combinations, and like the finest Girl Guide, Boy Scout, or both, is always prepared. That type of calculated thought we use, psychologists say, is left-brain thinking. It's linear. It's a problem solver. It organises our busy schedules. Let's face it,

---

22 *Whilst I'm encouraging your creative talents here, you need to know that creativity doesn't really happen when you're operating from the 'screw you' perspective. Nice try, though. Don't' stress, we'll shape you into something creative as we progress.*

the words strategic and analytical even sound rather clever. Surely, it's all we need to apply that moveable feast called 'the law' to the facts we're presented with.

But, wait! There's more! With your left brain comes a free right brain. No, not steak knives. A complete, right hemisphere of your brain. *"What's it good for?!"* you ask, already analysing a potential problem.

Back to school we go.

I have an interesting instructor for this one. Her name is Jill Bolte Taylor. She is a duly qualified neuroanatomist. Your left brain is now saying, *"Yes, she has a certificate with 'Neuroanatomist' on it, therefore she must know a good deal about neuro and anatomy."* Well, yes, that's true, but she also knows some special things about brains. Both the left and the right parts. Let me tell you her story.[b]

Jill decided to dedicate her career into researching severe mental illnesses. Her motivation was to understand more about her brother, who was diagnosed with schizophrenia. Specifically, her work at the time involved comparing the brains of those individuals who could be called normal control, and those diagnosed with schizophrenia and other similar disorders.

On the morning of 10 December 1996, a blood vessel in the left half of Jill's brain burst, and in the four hours that followed, whilst she realised she was having a stroke, she remained calm enough to proclaim how *"cool"* that experience was, given not many scientists get the opportunity to *"study their own brain from the inside out"*. I love this woman.

She explains that the left and right halves of the brain are completely separated. And that they process information completely differently, having, as she describes *"different personalities"*. In computing terms, because I know how you all just love a bit of IT, the left half operates like a serial processor and the right, being more like a parallel processor.

As the left side of her brain began to shut down, she was fortunate to glean some remarkable insights (an appropriate term) about the hemispheres' separate identities. The important distinction she makes, at first, is that the left side perceives you as a separate individual. It sees you, as you see yourself in the mirror, as being a solid form. An object. It allocates you neatly into a separate 'there I am' identifiable self.

From a time perspective, she noted that whilst the left brain enjoys linear time, it also lives all over the place – in the past, and in the future. It keeps talking to you about events which are long gone and random possibilities which might eventuate. All. Day. Long. Without reprieve. It natters to you about the world, describing it as you move through it. Like, *"What's the cat doing now?" "The washing machine ate the other sock again", "I really shouldn't eat that last piece of chocolate"*, and other such useful titbits for your listening pleasure during the day. Even though it's your voice of reason, categorising and organising, the type that lawyers need, it's also that annoying voice that takes over your life. So much so that you wish it would just shut up sometimes. It's a control freak that, with its constant time travel, is sometimes also an 'out of control' freak, always zooming you into images it creates from its Crystal Ball of Doom.

As Jill sunk deeper into losing the capacity of her more domineering left brain, she discovered that her right brain sees the world entirely differently. It thinks in pictures, and the information processed within the right side *"streams in simultaneously through all our sensory systems and explodes into this enormous collage of what this present moment looks like."* It lives in the present moment and sees everything as energy. The exact opposite to the way the left side sees things only in solid form. Jill then articulates the most magnificent view from our right brain, who sees us as:

> "*energy-beings connected to one another through the consciousness of our right hemispheres as one human family. And right here, right now, we are brothers and sisters on this planet, here to make the world a better place. And in this moment, we're perfect, we are whole and we are beautiful.*"

A few things I want to say about Jill's experience. Pretty 'mind blowing' evidence of what I was describing in Part II if you don't *mind* my saying so. Particularly, given she was perfectly conscious during this experience.

In case you hadn't considered this, her experiences also may explain to you why it is when you are all consumed by the depths of your favourite creative passion, like mowing the lawn, or making a batch of cookies, time, to you, does not exist. That's the unexplored right hemisphere of your brain getting some air time. Streaming exploding collages sound far more interesting than Crystal Balls of Doom, in my view.

In summary, there are two independent halves to our one brain. They seem like polar opposites. My overseer left says it's all about solid me and time is of the essence – so very lawyer of it. Whereas the more subservient right assures me I am sensory, I am everywhere and I seem to operate with a good deal of creative adjectives, and there is no time like the present. No time at all, in fact.

You're now thinking with your left brain. Oh dear, we better not let that right brain out, how do you charge in time increments if there's no concept of time?

I now pose the question, should we stick with what we trust and know, even if it thwarts us with thoughts we'd rather not be thinking?

Based on the evidence put before us by Jill Bolte Taylor, this might be how lawyers would approach the issue:

In the Matter of The Use of:

Brain v. Brain

[Supreme Court of Being, Year of Now, Unreported]

Counsel for the Left:

> *"The right brain is Out. Of. Control, Your Honour. It's emotional, subjective. Let's face it, no-one understands it. It's all creative, fluff and nonsense, sparkles and unicorns. We can't run a legal system without structure. Systems by their mere definition need a system. That's got left brain written all over it.*

> *"The evidence is solid, Your Honour. Ipso facto the left brain is superior. It's a tool we lawyers need. How can we possibly adjourn this hearing one more time if we have no idea of the concept of time?"*

Counsel for the Right:

> *"Well, Your Honour, the right brain exists, therefore it is.*

> *[Oh dear, realising the argument for the left brain has just been advanced, Counsel for the Right wipes brow and continues.]*

> *"What I mean to say, is I think therefore I am, which has been an age-old philosophical query, and lawyers really should be getting more in touch with their philosophical and creative side.[23] The right brain's value is that it operates outside the constraints of left-brain thinking. Without it nothing new would be created.*

---

23 *For those of you that read Part II, you can now see how that statement should really be stated in reverse. I am therefore I think. Just sayin'.*

"The left, whilst great at keeping court dates and using big, creative words, which I might add encroaches on my creative jurisdiction, I'll concede Your Honour, remains a tool."

Despite the jury's shock and surprise at that last remark, it appears the jury remains out in that case. We can't value one side of the brain over the other.

Jill Bolte Taylor's discovery that you have *"two cognitive minds"*, means that you can step into the perspective of one or the other any time you chose. It would seem realistic then, that at least from a more life-fulfilling point of view, if we were to at least tap into a little more of that right side, it could help us. A little less structure and a little more flow perhaps. *"A little less conversation, a little more action please."* Elvis said it. It must be true.

That said, you had chosen to be a lawyer. You must have had conviction about that career choice to undergo those countless hours of study. I imagine you weren't pondering too deeply about which side of your brain you were using as long as some of that information soaked in somehow and landed in correct sequence on your exam papers.

A huge investment.

What did you really hope to achieve? No matter which way you look at it, you either wanted to genuinely help people, gain recognition or both. Either way, from your perspective, you invested all that time and energy into training yourself to achieve what you perceived would bring you the most happiness, be it financial security, status, respect or service. You walked this path in the sincere belief it would open the door to your ultimate gratification. This, one could then reasonably deduce, would also amount to what you might have thought to be your life's purpose.

If you have convinced yourself that being a lawyer is, or should be, your life purpose, then we should probably consider what the words life and purpose mean when you stick them together. I will firstly assume, given that you're reading this, that you are alive. I will then logically conclude that there is some life in you. How much may depend largely on the next word. Purpose.

What is purpose? Especially when it's sitting right next door to the word life.

I recently saw a YouTube video created by Adam Liepzig.[c] Adam, for those of you who have not heard his name before, has produced many renowned films, is a speaker, writer and does other noteworthy things. People, it seems, like to hear what he has to say. The title of his video: 'Finding Your Life Purpose In 5 mins', caught my eye as a promising solution to my question. *Wow! Five minutes*, I thought. *I can locate my life purpose, and all will be well in just five easy listening minutes.* 12.7 million others thought so too. It must be a winner. I wondered what side of the brain you would use in this little exercise.

The watercooler version goes something like this:

Adam attended his 25-year college reunion tent party. Outside the noisy party tent, he made what he felt was an *"astounding discovery"*. Eighty percent of his classmates were unhappy with their lives. Eighty percent. That's a grown-up slice of the 'unhappy with life' pie. These unhappy ones bemoaned that they were now halfway through their lives and felt it was wasted. They had no idea what their life was all about. Clearly, a PhD in satisfaction was nowhere to be found on their list of accomplishments. The interesting thing was, these people went to Yale. They were privileged and highly educated. They wanted for nothing in a material sense. They held positions of power. To the outsider, they each had it all. Just goes to show, satisfaction does not of itself manifest in the form of 'materially privileged'.

He then investigated the 'happy' twenty percent of the group. They had studied things like literature, renaissance rhetoric, theatre, people and history. They had studied for the joy of learning. They didn't study for the sole purpose of attaining a specific job. They lived their lives expansively with the ups and downs but did not feel as though they'd wasted a single minute. From this short survey, he summarised that those who felt most successful were those that served others by changing people's lives. Engaging in the service of humanity was found to provide a deep connection with others.

He says that, for instance, if you write children's books you might say that you gave children awesome dreams. Or if you designed affordable apparel, you could claim that you helped people look and feel their best.

I pondered his observation for a moment and applied it to lawyers. As lawyers, we could say we help people through conflict. That would be agreeable and could certainly fit the mould of a 'fulfilling life purpose'. At first blush, the consensus would be that lawyers certainly do change people's lives. Whilst implied, I think Adam really needed to add to his formula the words, 'for the better', if you know what I mean *wink*.

Reading between the lines, Adam's little survey did highlight the distinct possibility, however, that being all left-brained and clever, having your path neatly mapped out with goals in clear view was not necessarily delivering the greatest life satisfaction. And by knowing the ending right at the beginning, whilst 'safe' has no real meaning. In the end. You're at the end. Before it even starts. There is no purpose to starting at the end.

To add to that conundrum, how do you get to look forward to something if there are only highlights? There needs to be low and dark before high and light can even exist. As human beings we are designed to have experiences. Whilst Adam's twenty percent really had no idea how life was going to pan out, it appears they were, at the very least, in touch with how they felt about things. They were the creative ones. Working with our feelings, a right-brained feature, seems to be an element necessary to make this life worthwhile. More than that, it implies the deep connection afforded by right-brained thinking helps you travel with others in your exploration of this life through the happy times and the not so happy times. You are *with* them; not just staring at them from the other side of a desk.

Let's play a little game with our food[24] to see how this could look.

Behind door 1, we have plain vanilla ice-cream. Let's begin by imagining that the smooth and un-besmirched vanilla ice-cream is your life. It's nice and, well... it's vanilla. There's not much going on here. Yes, there's flavour. But just one. No real texture to speak of. Each bite you take, you know what's going to happen next. Yes, I agree, nice for a while, but you can't live your whole life in the predictability state. It's just too predictable. There's no variety! In fact, there's nothing much at all. It's reliable. It's safe. It's so safe, it's beige. It's boring. How can boring add up to fulfilling?

Step behind door 2, and we have rocky road on offer. Rocky Road, complete with its lumpy bits of surprise. Let's imagine for a moment that those lumpy bits represent feelings that you have to face as you chomp in. Just so you know, I really don't like the glacé cherries. I'm going to pretend that you don't like them either. They'll represent the less than fun feelings. Let's just pretend, okay? Let's also pretend that our pink and white marshmallows, which are studded generously throughout our rocky road experience, are way yummier than vanilla ice-cream.

So here you have your life. It's represented by waves of thrilling

---

24 *I'm a grown-up now and I can do whatever I want.*

chocolate. That thrilling sumptuous chocolate surrounds fascinating lumpy bits. Chomp. Mmmm, ecstatic pieces of marshmallow. Chomp. A few nutty nuts go by. Chomp. Some fun coconut sprinkles... and, chomp. Those glacé cherries. *sad face* Chomp. Again, marshmallow surprise. There is no plan in there. They all happen, they taste great as a whole package, and you get to experience so much more than one flavour. By further embellishing my adjectivally dizzying highs and plummeting lows, you can make the lows lower and the highs seem higher. A roller coaster. The exact opposite of boring. Fulfilment right there. Surely you can't top that?

Votes are in. Polls have closed. Rocky Road takes it home![25] Let's face it, you just can't describe a nutty nut to someone if all you've experienced is vanilla.

Right brained sensory systems? Rocky roads? Doors? Choices? Sounds to me like the 'f' word is bubbling up for a serious viewing.

Feelings.

You knew they were in there. You've seen them in your clients. They've probably scared the hell out of you. Nonetheless, they do exist and I'd like you to be open to the idea that you may have found some genuine value and validity in exercising some right-brained thinking. But for those of you who remain doubtful, let's gather up some more research about it. Your left brain will think it's great fun.

We'll start by considering how it's possible, or even whether it's a worthwhile exercise for us to even bother connecting with our feelings when they have, for all intents and life purposes, been programmed out of us. The first valid reason springing to my mind is that you cannot connect with someone and their legal problems

---

25 *I counted the votes. There was one. It sure is fun when only my opinion matters.*

if you are viewing them like they are 'problems to be solved' rather than 'persons with feelings'. The irony here is you have to find your own feelings first before you can recognise them in others. Challenge accepted.

Inspiration for this task presented itself to me in a book which, invariably crossed my nutty nut embellished path, entitled *Search Inside Yourself*. Sounded deep, I thought, and could be just the ticket to prising open the impenetrable Suit. I was surprised to see it was written by a software engineer at Google called Chade-Meng Tan, 'Meng' for short. He was employee number 107 at Google and his self-imposed job title was *Jolly Good Fellow*. I liked him the most when I read that.

Meng introduced a course of the same name at Google in 2007, helping participants whilst using computing metaphors to take a look within as a solution to managing the stress associated with their work as engineers. In that course he was able to introduce the concept of mindfulness, cleverly woven under the guise of the term Emotional Intelligence. His guidance encouraged various ways for the engineers to perceive their feelings and emotions as they bubbled into existence. He received impressive feedback from participants, who reported it as giving greater substance to their jobs, and in turn their lives. He recounted one engineer having even sought to reduce his working hours so he could enjoy some quality time.[26] After enjoying said quality time, the employee's perspective on life improved and, wait for it, he got a promotion. There's a fine example of that whole cake and eat it too situation happening.

Meng has a fun approach to the topic and it's a book worth reading. I figured if he could get engineers into a state of cake-eating inner peace by understanding feelings packaged in a more sophisticated term like Emotional Intelligence, I could do the same for lawyers.

26 *Quality time: the time you get for yourself when you're not at work. Yes, it's a thing.*

Particularly, given my presumption that software engineers would probably have had the same attitude to the 'f' word as lawyers.

Emotional Intelligence.

Lovely words, and paired together sound more, well, intelligent and therefore appealing to an intelligent type of person. Please do not prove me wrong on this. It'd really be embarrassing. Let's face it, Meng tricked his group of engineers into meeting their right brains. I've already introduced you to yours, so we're way ahead on that front.

For the sake of this exercise, let's refer to right-brain thinking as regular thinking laced with Emotional Intelligence[27] (hereinafter referred to as 'EI'). EI is also referred to as EQ. This is to make it another 'thing' to measure your self-worth. Now you can see it has value. You might also be fascinated to learn that EI has now become a convincing rival to our old friend IQ. Now I've really piqued your interest, being up for a good argument and all. Let me run you through that again. EI = EQ vs IQ. Good math! Now we understand that. Let's break it down.

Back in the good old days you would sit an IQ test to see if you were a smart cookie. If the test revealed your inner Einstein, then you told everyone. If the test indicated otherwise, you criticised the test, pointing out its inadequacies and became a lawyer. Good job. Measuring your level of intelligence in this way was thought to be a good thing if you knew where to find the intelligence.

Before Meng's sneaky plot to inject engineers with feeling, Emotional Intelligence presented itself into the mainstream in 1995, in Daniel Goleman's book of the same name. As a journalist for the *New York Times* and psychologist, Goleman set out to unearth some wisdom in "*a guide to making sense of the senselessness*"

---

27 *I'll slowly wean you off the word intelligence, so all we'll have left to do is deal with emotion. It's part of the whole covert operation thing I have going.*

as a way of responding to the bad news infiltrating his life. Taking in newly-discovered scientific data on the value of emotions as a hopeful remedy, he noted that:

> "*These are times when the fabric of society seems to unravel at ever-greater speed, when selfishness, violence, and a meanness of spirit seem to be rotting the goodness of our communal lives. Here, the argument for the importance of emotional intelligence hinges on the link between sentiment, character, and moral instincts. There is growing evidence that fundamental ethical stances in life stem from underlying emotional capacities.*"[d]

From this, I appreciate his view that emotional expression is fundamental to community coherence. It is from the aspect of recognising the need for the presence of emotion as a 'hopeful remedy' that I take my stance.[28] Intelligent indeed.

Recall also that Jill Bolte Taylor recognised the importance of exercising our two states of mind. In applying a real-life example of such importance, let me talk about a recent shoe shopping experience of mine. Showcased before me, in Expensive Shoe Shop window, were the leopard-print shoes of glory. I am in two minds as to whether to buy those leopard-print shoes. A dilemma, I know. My right brain says, "*Oooh yes! I'd feel great in those*", but my left brain stoically points out, "*Are you sure you want them in beige, you already have three other shades?*".[29] Two valid and, dare I say it, intelligent perspectives of the one very serious issue.

From this example we can rightly see that IQ is recognised for its ability to measure general intelligence, such as evaluating whether you can logically own more than three shades of leopard-print

---

28 *Once again, picture me, hands on hips, cape dutifully flapping in the breeze... I do need to find out where that breeze is coming from.*

29 *Note to the uninitiated leopard-print shoe purchasers. Yes, they come in shades. Very. Important. Information.*

shoes. Assuming one's bank balance allows it, yes, you can. But *should* you? This is why it's been conceded that the IQ test is not as appropriate in defining mainstream intelligence as first thought.

The recognised limitations to the IQ test, as foreshadowed by Goleman, arise in its incapacity to measure distinct qualities such as creativity, morality, practical skills, virtue and character. EQ, from right-brained thinking, as you can see from my fine shoe shopping example, fills in those blanks. With feelings, and dare I say, virtue. There would be no point in executing my purchase solely from a calculated perspective. You must therefore have EQ + IQ to be the full picnic. Right brain plus left brain = whole brain.

We've checked out why it may be rather necessary to add a little right-brained thinking into our lives. Creativity. Feeling good. Fulfilment of purpose. Marshmallows. We've given our left brain some critique on it's rather shallow but necessary existence. It's a great tool and time keeper when you have its Crystal Ball of Doom under control. It's allowed us to travel this far, despite leaving us not as fulfilled as we'd like, with its tendency to view the world in separation.

Given that saving the best part for last is always a great idea, there's a little more that I need to bring to your attention. You may now appreciate I have a great intelligence for shoe shopping and let no-one tell you otherwise. Until, of course, there's a sale on. In the frenzy, my otherwise intelligent mind turns to scribble. So yes, having a high intelligence is impressive until someone upsets your proverbial apple cart, then even the most intelligent of us will do some silly things.

It may, or may not, come as a surprise to you, but the only reason we choose to do anything at all is because it makes us *feel* better. There's that whole emotional thing again. Let's face it, if general intelligence was the ruler of my being, I would sensibly choose sugar-free mung bean meringue for dessert over that delicious piece of salted caramel chocolate. Instead, faced with that choice, when other hidden factors are at play, my very own brain hijacks me and takes me to the dark side.

Why then do these silly things happen to otherwise intelligent humans?

It all stems from the random behaviour of a little nutty almond-shaped contraption located right behind our eyes called the amygdala. The amygdala is a little firecracker! Daniel Goleman was one of the first people to recognise that it can hijack your emotions entirely. You are right in the middle of an intelligent conversation and then someone mentions the colour of your tie in an off-handed way, *"Like your magenta tie."* BAM! You're off! Ranting about the price of ties. In swung your amygdala like Tarzan, except the exact opposite of Tarzan because you are really not the hero of this story. You're looking more like his friend cheetah, with a magenta tie – a bit silly.

> *"The amygdala can house memories and response repertoires that we enact without quite realizing why we do so because the shortcut from thalamus to amygdala completely bypasses the neocortex. This bypass seems to allow the amygdala to be a repository for emotional impressions and memories that we have never known about in full awareness."*[x]

Trouble can just swing right on in, without permission. This can be a scary concept to the uninitiated.

Let me explain.

CHAPTER

2

Living in full colour

You have no doubt seen, at one time or another, all those funky colouring books for grown-ups. They sold them to us as being therapy or something similar. Whilst that fad has come and gone (I guess therapists didn't miss out on too much), I think we can all agree that there is something about colouring-in that brings our inner child out to play. I can see mine now, jumping with excitement. I know my small self would sit there for hours, absorbed completely in bringing a few empty dark lines to colourful life. A picture, thankfully, that I did not have to draw. No self-judgement here.

Now I'm a grown-up, I'm happy to report that I can now colour in properly. I can stay in the lines neatly, and shade with anal precision. And, at long last, I can finally afford to buy one of those very expensive wooden boxes of pencils complete with the full array of colours, possessing shades like 'wild cerise' and 'molten puce'. So exciting! The big box. It's orderly. It's satisfying.

Imagine for a moment that you had a scene you wanted to colour in. Imagine that scene is of a forest. A tropical rainforest. I just love the tropics, not to live in, but to visit when my Melbourne winters get too sad for me to bear. The tropics are dotted with plenty of chill-thawingly vibrant colours, perfect for our colouring-in project.

The thought excites me so much that I can feel the tropical warmth spilling out onto the page. Before me are the lined etchings of what will form luscious trees, birds, and flowers. Shades of green, red, orange, yellow and blue awaiting my undivided attention. The whole rainbow. You get the idea. All the colours are here and, as the saying goes, I am going to *"colour myself happy!"*.

I start colouring in some flowers. The birds. There's a rainbow as relief to the azure blue sky. No, there are no clouds, this is a happy picture. Let's not get technical. The brilliant colours as they animate the page excite me most. I'm saving my trees for last because they're the biggest area to colour and, whilst I can choose from assorted shades of green, green is needed to complete the majority of the project, so I decide I'll use my greens to finish off.

For days on end I go about colouring. Carefully. Neatly. Dare I say it, skilfully. Bringing to life this work of art.

Then... wait! Hang on! Panic sets in. Where are the greens? I upend the box. Pencils everywhere. The greens are missing from the box. How can I colour the rainforest without green? There will be a blank space. Right. In. The. Middle. Of my rainbow. There's no disguising that one, my friends. I just can't complete the picture.[30]

Where did the green go?

Whilst I'll keep it brief, this is in fact a long story. Probably as long as your life, minus up to about eight or so years.

I'll give you a clue.

Peter Pan.

Yes, his rather snazzy little outfit is green. Right down to his tights. Close one. But that's not the answer. I can't finish colouring in

---

30 *For all you other accidental yogis out there, the missing green is a nod to the heart chakra. Just thought I'd throw that one in for you guys.*

with his tights, though a novel experience it would be. It's all about Peter's shadow. He loses it. The shadow, I mean. And when he finds it again, Wendy sews it firmly back on. He is now one happy mythical boy, complete with shadow.

He is relieved to have his shadow right in a place where he recognises it and can keep a keen eye on it. This is a great start. But it's dark, this shadow. It doesn't reflect his green outfit at all.

It's a long shot, and playful, but if I point over there and your eyes follow I will distract you just enough so I can seam (pardon the pun) neatly into talking about our nemesis, the human shadow.

It's real.

It can stalk you.

Even at night.

Some people have more than one, and others so many that it's a crowd, or a party, depends on how you like to look at it.

Enter the shadow...

I like listening to a whole lot of interesting people talk about a whole lot of interesting things. Among one of those interesting people was a woman called Teal Swan. She calls herself a spiritual catalyst. Probably a bit too much for your legal minds to grapple, but that's her title. I know you probably preferred *Jolly Good Fellow,* but we'll just accept, in a loving way, that's what her label is. I became fascinated by some of Teal's work, which she called the Completion Process. So, I packed myself up and underwent her practitioner's course. The training was an intense few days shared with other participants learning how we can heal ourselves from the traumas carried with us since we were young. I learned this was more commonly referred to as shadow work.

Seeking a bit more grounded and historical information on this very new-to-me topic, I found that the human shadow in this form was first coined in modern society by influential psychiatrist Carl Jung back around the early 1900s. Jung was creating a process which he called individuation, which involved integrating the layers of one's psyche to create a wholeness within. This had the result of revealing who we truly are. As he looked deeply within the human condition, he found there was a part of our personality that remained suppressed in the unconscious part of ourselves, which he described as the human shadow. A part of our personality had effectively gone MIA, much like my green pencils.

The unconscious part of us is also that part which does things on autopilot. It likes to mend our sliced finger after we've been working with our less-than-talented onion chopping skills. It's the part that beats our heart and breathes our breaths for us. It has many other worthwhile skills too. But our unconscious, or subconscious, as it is also fondly known, is a secret controller. It goes to work without your conscious knowledge. That, my friends, is why it is called our un-conscious. So, if we add that all up, our shadow is a piece of our personality working undercover to secretly control us. And it's green. Not really... I made that up (it was my creative shadow at work, as we go on, you will see that I really need to rein it in).

But in my inimitable way of discovering things, it seemed the human shadow has been a staple of humanities' glitches in the world of the shaman, way before Jung pronounced its existence. And this was indeed a claim Jung made himself.

Shamanism.

Sounded mystical to me. Thought I'd better take a look. Well, it couldn't hurt now, could it? It's all in the name of research, I rationalised. It is said that shamanism originated in Siberia, that being the case, there nevertheless appears to be no universally recognised definition of the term. It's also practised in many cultures around world. The earliest record of the term shaman that I could find dates back around two and a half thousand years. Suffice to say that the practise still exists today, so one could logically conclude that something must have been working for them to sustain such a following. Let's face it, the notion that the world was flat had its 15 minutes of fame, whereas shamanism remains in current practise and has a resume of around 2.5 millennia or perhaps even longer. This makes me think this idea has roots.

Jung aligned his thinking in this area with traditional shamanism. His experiences led him to understand shamans to be great healers because they have been wounded to such a degree that their dismembered pieces had to have been *slowly collected and put together again with the greatest care*.[f] Mircea Eliade, a recognised authority on shamanism, also points out *"the shaman, is not only a sick man; he is, above all, a sick man who has been cured, who has succeeded in curing himself"*.[g]

Moving forward on the timeline, I found a modern shaman. In her book called, *Soul Retrieval: Mending the Fragmented Self,* Sandra Ingerman says from a shaman's customary view, that *"whenever we experience trauma, a part of our vital essence separates from us in order to survive the experience by escaping the full impact of the pain"*.[h] This modern perspective correlates neatly with Jung's view that the darker aspects within the human condition arise from those suppressed parts of our personality. Even the traditional shamans of Central and North Asia say that illnesses arise from *"corruption or alienation of the soul"*.[i]

I want you to know that Sandra, whilst being a trained shaman also holds a master's degree in counselling psychology. Her experience taught her that *"psychotherapy works only on the parts of us that are 'home'"*. This means that you have to have all the colours in your pencil box; or, in other words, all aspects of yourself need to be present and accounted for before you should go on any further self-improvement quest. It was at this point she turned toward the shamanic principles referred to as soul retrieval. Soul retrieval, whilst sounding drastic, is simply a method used by shamans to bring you into alignment with all aspects of your truest self. To bring your parts home, in Sandra's words. This is useful if you have a trained shaman to complete the process for you.

Then I happened upon the traditional Hawaiian shamans who used a method some have referred to as *ho'oponopono*,[31] which essentially means 'to make right'. It was seen that you needed to seek forgiveness for your transgressions else you would fall ill. It was traditionally a process invoked to resolve family or community conflict via a process of forgiveness and reconciliation. The idea being, everyone in the community possesses a level of responsibility for all its members. A type of restorative justice.

A modern version of the *ho'oponopono* was brought into existence by Morrnah Nalamaku Simeona in 1976. She was was a respected *kahuna lapa'au*, or healer. She wanted people to be able to use a method to heal themselves, given the traditional method required community participation.[32] To do this, she worked with what she described as the three parts of the mind, the conscious, the subconscious and the superconscious *"to resolve and remove traumas from the 'memory banks'."*[j]

Our subconscious operates as an automated function within our bodies. It has readily been described in computer speak as being our internal operating system, which runs many simultaneous

---

31 *You think that's a mouthful? Try saying Humuhumunukunukuapua'a, Hawaii's State fish. Lucky that fish is not a lawyer. Fancy signing that name 86 times a day.*

32 *Whilst not within the scope of this book, I am firmly of the opinion that the traditional Hawaiian ho'oponopono, should be explored in greater depth in the realms of community responsibility in conflict resolution.*

programs. The shadow aspect of ourselves has been identified as a glitch in the corresponding program. These malfunctions are those relating to your memories and emotions. The green pencil is stuck and jamming up the whole system. It needs to be found and wriggled free to express its fullest green glory in every shade. Until this occurs, you can only view the world without green. Yes, you can mix blue and yellow, but it's not green coming through to you in its purest form. In other words, you can fake some tears but are you really expressing your sadness?

The shadow, as we will see later, messes with your perception. It prevents you from seeing the world in full colour.

Perception – it's all in the way you look at it

How we engage in our lives is all about our perception of the world around us. I'll take a step to the left of the shadow for a moment to provide a simple example of how perceptions can be formed.

Say I was bitten by a dog when I was four years old. A big dog. You, on the other hand, could ride your big dog around the house. We are now all grown-ups. I come over to your house to visit, and I see your big dog, all teeth and drooly, lurking behind you. Yes, lurking. That's what I see, teeth, drool and lurk. I won't come inside. You think I'm completely irrational. You see your dog as all teethy-smiles and comforting. Polar opposites. You will not get me in there. My younger experience with dogs will render me terrified of dogs for the rest of my life.

That is what we call a differing perception. From my eyes plays-out completely different scenery in comparison to the view from your eyes. Yet, they are both 'real' perceptions. What you see is real to you and what I see is very real to me. Incidentally, this is why the reliability of witness testimony has been questioned. I have my serious face on when I say that, if nothing else, the concept of individual perception is vital information that I need you to take with you.

We all see the world based on our own past life experiences. We apply laws we've self-imposed to the facts at hand. When there's a situation unfolding before us we run that scenario through the data-base in our subconscious and out spits a result: our personal point of view.

The lurky dog example demonstrates that a conscious fear has developed from a past experience, that experience created a law – dogs are scary – and that law has remained firmly intact. That example reveals a *conscious* fear arising from a conscious experience. This is in direct contrast to developing our shadow, which is unconscious. Consciously we can remember how we developed our fear of dogs. Whereas, the shadow likes to lurk too, but in the darkness where it's not easily recognised. Shadows equally shape how we perceive our world. It is in the darkness of not knowing what we don't know, which is the puzzle to be solved here.

Formation of the shadow

It's now reasonable to want to know how you came upon this thing called a shadow, and why someone like Peter Pan would want something as nasty as all that sewn back on.

How do they form?

I'll now shed a light on how shadows became recognised as a scary thing. Well, not if there's light, because there will be no shadow. Anyway, bear with me. I am going somewhere with this.

Just so you can see the connection, that firecracker amygdala of yours has a role to play in the formation of shadows. Whilst its essential role is to govern your ability to feel certain emotions and perceive them in other people, it's also the meeting place for many of your bodily sensory informers to let you know you're in danger. It lets you know when it's time to dive for cover.

It keeps you safe.

Before you donned your legal Suit of Armour, you may have viewed the world a little differently. You might, for instance, have been one of those students that viewed a career in law as your ticket to save the world. You felt like you would at last be recognised for the honourable intentions you've carried with you all your life. If you're not that person, then you may fit the category of the 'other' type of law student. Some of you envisioned a legal career as an identity to be formed. One described as 'Partner' of Legal Eagle Law Firm on your short-form-identity placard of a business card. Complete with corner office. That's ok too. We all want something out of this life.

Whilst they are indeed life goals, recall we also talked about careers as forming part of your life's purpose. And that life had to have some meaning to it, some real flavours to be worthwhile. More so, those flavours had something to do with the experiencing of feelings.

The point is, when you entered law school, you probably weren't at that time, terribly well acquainted with the most authentic level of yourself. Hang in there, students of the saviour variety. I'm not raining on your 'world saving' parade at all.[33] I'm just giving everyone a little peek into how everyone's thinking processes have been moulded over time. Recall you were born perfect. And a little time has certainly elapsed since the miracle of your birth.

Backing up a little, it is fundamental that you do remember, or if your memory is bad, just trust me when I say, that you were born as

---

[33] That you recognised the world needs saving is a great aspect of you, if it's for the right reasons. And you need to pay attention, as what I am showing you will help you with your mission. The world needs saving from its collective shadow. But that's another story.

perfection itself. Some of you still think you are. And you are right. In a sense. Or in essence, actually. On the day you were born, there were no prior influences impressed upon the person you were. Life was pure and simple. You cried. You pooped. You cried some more. Then in no time at all you performed the part the adults were waiting for... the giggle. Baby giggles are the Best. Thing. Ever.

That was all that was expected of you. For a short time. Before you knew it, a list of anticipated milestones was rolled out before you. You had performance targets you were required to meet. By your first birthday you really should have been walking. By two, you should know your alphabet. By four, you were supposed to be able to tie a shoe lace. But the biggest 'should' of all, was you should be good and fit neatly into the identity your parents had envisioned for you. You were there for the moulding, and some of you were even placed in your care-giver's capable hands to be pummelled into the requisite cookie-cutter shape.

Entry-level planet Earth for us humans is as a pure blank canvas. The trouble is, it was your parents and carers that thought they could draw your portrait. It is you as the individual, however, who is the only one possessing that power. Like a salmon, you inherently know which stream of life you're going to swim up when the time comes. You were born with an innate ability to uncover your own path. For yourselves. As small, innocent creatures, you needed to be able explore the world around you and to develop the talents that are inherently yours. You were born containing access to all the colours to create a masterpiece. You are the creation and the creator. You are designed to experience this life to its fullest.

Humans have five senses designated to achieving that life-fulfilling intention. Along with some other great concealed features, like feelings and intuition, we come into this life slowly drawing that picture which represents the creation that is us. The creation that we will develop into, one colour at a time.

It wasn't much help to you if your parents placed their large hand over your small one forcing you to trace out a lawyer when you were holding tightly onto the green pencil labelled gardener. This would frustrate you. Your shadows first come into existence when you repress your vulnerability and authenticity in situations where you are unable to express how you genuinely feel about a situation.

You are born a sentient being. Feelings are the way you experience the world until you're old enough to intellectualise and rationalise the behaviour around you. For some of you that takes a long time. Feelings are essential to your growth as a human being. They are elemental in creating connections with others. If you can't feel something you have no experience of it. How do you know you hate broccoli if you've never tried it? For me, I never liked the 'idea' of yoga and fortunately for me it literally took a bloody accident to get me to try it. I feel great practising yoga. That experience changed my entire life. It opened a doorway into myself, without which, we would not be having this little chat.

In the following examples, I describe why it is vitally important to have the full set of feelings at your ready.

The shadow of the hidden choice (control)

Having not spoken of my beloved friend chocolate for a while, I think its high time I created another tasty scenario. Bring in Aunt Rosie, my favourite fictional aunt. With a name like Rosie, she's got to be a favourite.

She pops over for afternoon tea, resplendent with her signature chocolate cake. She sets it down on the coffee table and turns her back to draw over a chair. Your nimble two-year-old self rushes in and grabs a handful of that delicious oozy cake. After all, it was beckoning you to do so. You're a feisty one. You have chocolate cake pasted everywhere. Some even reaches your mouth. Mmmmmm.

Chocolate.

Your mother yells at you. To an extent annoyed by your chocolatey hand prints on her beige sofa, but more so, covertly jealous of her sister's fine cake-making skills. You had no idea, but your mother always felt she could never measure up to her sister. She didn't become the baker her mother wanted her to be.[34] The baker that her sister is. *"See that chocolate cake"*, she warns you, *"I'm telling you it's terrible cake. No, you can't have any more! Chocolate is no good for you. We eat orange mousse in this family. We grow oranges. That's what's on offer and you'll like it too."*

Try as you might, you discover you don't like mousse, let alone orange mousse. You eat the mousse. You grimaced as you swallowed its slimy texture. You had to do it. That was all this household offered. Without it, you would not survive.

This may seem trivial, but it is imperative to understand. You rely on the adults in your life to love you and to keep you safe. Your small self understands that without the adults in your life to love, care for and protect you, you will not survive. You do all you can to ensure that you receive that love.

Love.

Soak that word in. When you are young, your instincts move you in the direction of anything that ensures you receive love. You do whatever it realistically takes to earn the love of those who should be caring for you.

Knowing that to remain in your carer's love zone, to remain safe and survive in this family, you 'embrace' orange mousse and sensibly stuff down your desire for chocolate. You learn to squash your own desires for anything at all really. The bottom line in this

---

34 *You might have now guessed that this is mother's shadow of "I am not good enough" taking charge.*

situation is, you have just been told that you don't know what's good for you, and to make your own choices will spell disaster. For the approval of all that matters to you, you proceed on in life to become an orange grower. All the while, your authentic-self arrived into this world with the blueprint to be a baker. Of all things, chocolate.

Having lived a good part of your existence as an orange grower, one day you secretly discover that you might really have a talent for all things chocolate. Eating it. Creating delicate masterpieces with it. You keep this in the closet so as not to offend your orange-centred family. After all, you trained to be an orange grower, and that's all you know how to do.

What will tend to happen now is people will keep showing up in your life as talented bakers. You will attract them time and again and they will *annoy* you with their chocolatey skills that they flaunt in front of you. You may also find that because you were unable to make your own choices, you often feel dissatisfied with your life as you were unable to live it as your authentic-self.

Not only will your shadow pop up in the form of such 'annoying' people, you may also recognise other tell-tale signs. For instance, you may find yourself being told you're a controlling person. Or you may attract other controlling people into your life. There may also be some other emotional and physical disorders you will manifest. I will give the latter topic some clarification further on.

In this example, we are holding onto the subconscious self-limiting belief that we are unable to decide things for ourself, and that we have no control over our life. Of course, this is not true. We just believe it is. Beliefs form part of our perception of life and so are very real to us. We firmly fixed that belief in place when we were two years old to protect ourselves. To dutifully be and do what we were told was our means of acceptance and, in turn, survival.

To resolve our shadow aspects, we will need to learn to take back the controls, but of our inner world. We need to put the boundaries back in place. We need to be able to say I don't want this. I want that instead. The two year old in this story lost that ability the moment the part allowing choice-making was suppressed. Stuffed down. Tucked away neatly. Never to see the light of day again, in... The Shadow.

> *Shadows are the aspects, or parts of us,*
> *that we have disowned for fear of missing*
> *out on being loved and accepted.*

The shadow of worthlessness (I am stupid)

Imagine for a moment that when you were growing up, you were a bit on the clumsy side. As a result, one of your parents used to tease you by calling you 'Dopey'. Even though this was teasing, you knew it was a real criticism. You soon learned that appearing stupid was not cool. In fact, to your small mind it meant rejection from this outwardly-appearing clever family. To hide your perceived 'stupidity' from your family and indeed your external world, you excel at school and attain a PhD in rocket science. When people look up the word 'serious' in the dictionary, your picture is right there.

Despite certificates with PhD written all over them as clear evidence to the world that you are in fact clever – being the exact opposite of stupid – for some reason unbeknownst to you, you hold onto an inkling that people still view you as stupid. You still believe somewhere at the core of your being that people are testing your intelligence.

You begin to realise something is going awry with you after someone innocently asks, "*Oh, what do you think the weather will be like this weekend?*" You snap back with "*How the bleep should I know? Do you think I'm a meteorologist?*" You've just defended yourself over a weather question, all the while contemplating your need for another certificate with Meteorologist written on it. Really, you just did that?

Well, you felt stupid for not knowing the answer to a question. You perceive the world by wearing sunglasses that filter it all into 'everyone thinks I'm stupid'. You see that everyone appears to be attacking you when the fact is, they are not. They're thinking about the weather, whereas in your corner of the world lurks a shadow called 'I am stupid'. It repeatedly puts you in situations that challenge your *belief* of that, *"I am not acceptable unless I seem smart"*. But you are already smart. You just cannot see that with those dark, shadowy sunglasses on.

In the previous example, essentially what's happening is, you are running a programme maintaining a self-limiting belief that says: *"I am not lovable unless I have a lot of certificates telling the world I am clever"*. From where you sit, being seen as clever means people will love and accept you. You are seeking external validation from the certificates, yet your shadow keeps popping up to say otherwise. The shadow says: *"I am here to let you know that feeling stupid is in fact a valid feeling. It belongs to you. Own it."*

Yes, own it!

That may sound counterintuitive to many of you. You might just be relieved to know that owning all aspects of yourself is a prerequisite to becoming the complete set. The whole human. And not one of us is exempt from displaying stupidity now and then. My personal favourites are leaving the iron on, or forgetting where I left my carkeys ... to name a few socially acceptable ones.

In the above scenario, stupidity wanted to be known as a valid and acceptable aspect. Until each aspect is embraced, it will keep presenting itself for your undivided attention. You cannot achieve any state of peace while all that's going on for you.

Seeking out the shadow

Importantly, the trouble is, as I fore-shadowed[35] in the analogies above, the shadow won't be silenced. It haunts you. It keeps popping its mysterious darkness up in one way or another until you pay attention to it. We need to recognise those shadowy parts of us so that we can address them. It's clear we need to go sunny-side up on it, and as Jung succinctly states that:

> *"One does not become enlightened by imagining figures of light, but by making the darkness conscious."*

Here he is saying external help won't cut it. We need to get out our torch and shine the light right onto the darkness. For ourselves. Dark can't exist where there is light. Good news.

Fine. You have a torch. At the ready. But the next question is, where do you shine it? The challenge for us is, as Daniel Goleman states, we are seeking to locate *"emotional impressions and memories that we have never known about in full awareness."* That is sometimes the biggest issue for us. How can we know what we don't know?

How do we get the green back in our palette? We need the full colour spectrum before we can head out and create our work of genius. How do we find our green pencil when we don't even know where to look? How do you even know it's green that you're missing?

The first logical question would then be, do I have a shadow?

That's a capital YES for all of us, I'm afraid. Not one of us escaped childhood unscathed by something. It's unavoidable. Some shadows are easy to find and deal with, others are so deep and complex that it takes a very patient and self-compassionate person to even want to go looking. Some of us have even hidden them under lock and key. But when things are continually not panning

---

35 *It had to be done.*

out in the way you'd hoped, that may just be the motivation you need to start the detective work.

The first indication that there may be a shadow loitering in your life is when you notice feelings of unusual discomfort about those unpleasant situations that keep entering your life. Discomfort in the form of being repelled by a person or people, or their actions. Each instance where you have a strong, lingering negative reaction to a situation, you need to check in to try and objectively see what's going on. That's not as easy as it sounds. Most of us tend to look at the dramas around us as problems that other people are causing us. We take the view that, if only they'd do the right thing then none of this would happen. We generally see others as the problem. But as Dr Ihaleakala Hew Len, who was one of Morrnah Simeona's students, observes, *"Have you ever noticed, when there's a problem, you're always there?"*.

We can see everyone else delivering up their skilfully-crafted chocolate cakes or ostentatiously provoking you with their certificate-filled walls in our direction, and it makes us wild. We become annoyed over and over again. Yet we don't really know why. When you find that people are really getting under your skin, your shadow is staring you right in your face and it's waving to you.

How awesome!

You recognised it exists. Yes, the box of pencils did come with green. They're just reflected outside the box. It's helpful to appreciate that we need to think outside the box when it comes to locating our shadows.

The second question is, where do you find them?

You need to hunt out where the green pencils first got lost so you can collect them and put them right back where they belong. Within the box. The majority of our shadows were formed when we were young, but often we have no idea when. 'Usually', disassociated aspects of ourselves were created, by us, at some point in our childhoods. Note my emphasis here is on the word 'usually'.

I particularly want to assure you at this point, that this is not about blaming those who raised us. This is not a blame game. In fact, I think as we're forgiving them, given they have their own shadows formed from their own childhoods, I think we should secretly thank them. My opinion is that a deeper meaning should be attributed to the reasons our shadows have formed, and I truly believe they have gifts to offer us. Yes, I did say gifts. Rest assured I, too, reflected over my parenting prowess for the past 21 years with some grimaces.

Who we are today is a result of ancestral lines of behaviour. The reason for this, I believe, arises from the ideas I put forth in Part II.[36] Further, Daniel Foor, who holds a PhD in psychology, submits that we can even access the wellness within our lineages to effect positive shifts in our lives, given that some of our shadows can be inherited. The beautiful news is that you are the one holding the power to change things for your entire life moving forward.

The power is within you.

Let's go hunting for those green pencils. Outside the box. In the mirror.

---

36 *That is, our challenges are placed before us for our growth and we all have a sneaky hand in designing them.*

There is an 'I' in conflict...

... just like there is an 'I' in mirror. Clever, aren't I?

You may have just gone all light bulb and "*aha!*" on me and figured out that it's the people around you, the people that you find most annoying, who are the key to finding your shadows. Bless their dark cotton socks.

There will be more than one.

More than one person, and more than one shadow, that is. And there is more than one way of recognising them. But one sure fire way to find out the nature of your most prominent subconscious self-limiting beliefs is by sincerely delving into an examination of your relationships with others.

Remember my reference to Einstein's take on matter? Matter constitutes those seemingly solid items in your life that decorate your day. Your couch. Your phone. Your bottle of red wine. Even you. Einstein pronounced that all those things, and every single other thing is all just energy. Energy operates at various frequencies. Low and slow, high and buzzy and all frequencies in between. For those of you that weren't physics geeks in school like me, we can also refer to these frequencies as vibrations. One of my other favourite scientists, Nicola Tesla, notes: "*If you want to find the secrets of the universe, think in terms of energy, frequency and vibration.*" You know I love a good secret. That's where Einstein's equally brilliant mind intersects. This part of his quote is really important: "*Match the frequency of the reality you want and you cannot help but get that reality.*"

Sounds a little like the law of attraction, doesn't it? You know, that funny little craze that swept everyone up as being the sure road to riches. Rhonda Byrne wrote about it in 2006, in *The Secret.*[37] You can have whatever you want? Yes, you can. The general view has been, simply think about what you want enough and it's yours. But I've learned that's not the whole story. The law of attraction is real nonetheless. Einstein's view on matter is the key to why the law of attraction doesn't manifest your ideal dreams by just thinking it to be so.

Einstein talked about matching the frequency to the reality that you want. Before I go further, I need to provide you with a very brief explanation of these so-called frequencies. On this topic, I have some scientific research to offer which has been recently proclaimed by Dr Joe Dispenza. As a science nut and a huge fan, I'll give you some of the creds on Dr Joe. He is a researcher in the fields of neuroscience, epigenetics, and quantum physics. He uses that knowledge to help people heal themselves of illnesses, chronic conditions, and even terminal diseases so they can enjoy a more fulfilled and happy life. He has partnered with other scientists to perform extensive research on the effects of meditation, including epigenetic testing, brain mapping with electroencephalograms (EEGs), and carries out individual energy field testing. I go on about his qualifications because I feel as a scientist, he has made real evidentiary impact into fields that others fear to tread. He truly needs to be acknowledged for this.

In his book entitled *Becoming Supernatural: How Common People Are*

---

37 *No doubt a nod to Tesla.*

Doing The Uncommon, published in 2017, he demonstrates that it's scientifically possible for you to attain an internal peaceful state irrespective of the drama in your external environment. Further, you can influence the state of your external environment based on the status of your internal environment. There's the whole mirror thing again.

What's going on inside of you will influence what's going on outside of you.

Dr Joe has formulated a helpful table of frequencies that have been measured, relating to differing emotional states. Elevated emotions such as bliss, freedom, love, and joy, have been measured at high frequencies. Go higher up the scale and the closer together the wiggly lines get. Whereas at the other end of the scale, we have the slower frequencies of fear, right down to the bottom of the list where we have the survival emotions of pain and lust. The lower you go on the frequency scale, the lower the height of the waves are, and the further apart. I imagine if you were to get below the lowest frequency it would be a flat line and you would be dead!

Moving back to the idea of making our dreams a reality.

Based on Dr Joe's frequency measurements, if we are feeling happy and lovable, we are vibrating at a high frequency. High frequencies tune us into the good things we are looking for.[38] On that basis, in line with the thinking offered up by *The Secret*, all you need to do is think a happy yachting thought and you should be a clear vibrational match to that 35 metre yacht you want to moor off the Amalfi coast for your spring holidays. Easy.

It is all well and good to *consciously* think blissful thoughts about things that we want. However, remember there's that *other* part of us called our subconscious. It harbours those rather undesirable

---

38 *For my Part II fans, I'm purposefully toning this down. It's source energy I'm really referring to here.*

fragments called shadows. Those shadows are self-limiting beliefs. Self-limiting beliefs are also energy. They resonate at the lower end of the frequency scale; not the happy, chill kind of vibe endorsed by hippies, or me.

For instance, say your father left your family and took all the money. It left your mother sad. You might quickly understand money's value to equal pain. You associate it with many feelings including sadness, abandonment, loneliness and powerlessness. To be seen as a strong little trooper for your mother, and so as to keep yourself safe to your last remaining caregiver, you then repress those feelings. They are also too much to bear. You will therefore have programmed within you a self-limiting belief that money is to be avoided. You think it's bad and as such causes you real pain.

These associations and beliefs remain within your subconscious and will vibrate at the same low frequency as pain. Your subconscious self is therefore not a total match to your very valid yacht desire. It is saying no, you do not fully match this. Therefore, you will not get your yacht as easily as you might have had you dealt with that disowned part of yourself.

These principles illustrate that connectedness thing I'm trying to get you to see. Due to our fundamental nature being energy, we are connected to all things and to each other at differing frequencies. If you want another fun analogy, think of a tuning fork. A common tuning fork sounds the note of A which vibrates at 440 hertz of frequency. If you have tuning forks of the same frequency nearby, they'll begin to vibrate too. Remove that fork from the original space, and the remaining forks will continue to vibrate.

In an everyday kind of scenario, this could translate to a setting where you have a room full of people at a show. In comes the warm-up guy. He gets the crowd all buzzing and leaves. His high vibe has an influence on the vibe of the audience. Despite him leaving the room, you still feel happy. Similarly, if you have someone who's on a downer walk into your party, you feel the mood drop. AKA the party pooper. The wet blanket. Extremes in vibe tend to have that effect on others long after they've left the building. Yes, Elvis was one person who could leave a blazing trail of energy behind him. In fact, I think that energy is still in existence now. *"Thank-you very much!"*

Similar to our yacht example, a person possessing a shadow with a lower frequency on the scale will attract people carrying the same vibe. They might look all happy-go-lucky on the surface, but within their subconscious is a similar low vibe, hence the attraction. This is valuable information as I will explain later.

To summarise. You are consciousness energy. Some of the energy that should be in the light of your consciousness is buried in the shadows. It's buried within your unconscious or subconscious – the automated parts of you. Those automated subconscious parts are operating programs that give off a certain vibe. In the world of energy, like the tuning forks, you will tune into someone who's operating at the same frequencies. You will attract people and experience things with the same vibe.

Why do we tune in to the low vibes?

As an added bonus, if your subconscious is trying to be heard, you will gravitate toward those experiences which highlight your repressed feelings. In fact, so much so that Dr Bruce Lipton PhD, a leading voice in cell biology and mind-body medicine asserts that:

> *"When it comes to sheer neurological processing abilities, the subconscious mind is more than a million times more powerful than the conscious mind."*[k]

Any wonder why the shadow can run the show and take you down without your permission.

But what if I just try really, really hard to change?

You think to yourself, fine, I'll just make a conscious choice to change myself. I'll smile more. I'll listen. I'll show empathy. You might as well also say, I'll win the lottery too. From what Dr Lipton said, you have to really go ahead and do some serious work on your conscious mind to make any progress. One million times more work. That sounds like an impossible workout to me.

The question really is, what are you trying to change? And how can you change if you have no idea what that could be? What you know to be real is just a simulation of your inner reality, and a culmination of predictions you've made based upon past events. You think you are an amiable sort. Your vibe is right up there on the scale of being up. But you seem to attract the grumpy ones. Oh, they start out all happy but soon enough, grumpy face is what you're looking at. How does it all go so rapidly downhill? How can I change from being more agreeable than I am? How far 'up' the scale do I need to go? Up is not the direction of choice in this instance.

It's 'in' that's the only 'in' place to be in this life.

Before I get to 'in', I assure you that I engaged in some inquisitorial pondering of my very own. I have always loved the quote: *"be the change you want to see in the world"* by Mahatma Gandhi. I think everyone's heard it before. It's short, succinct, and makes me feel like I could change the world by just saying it.

But the quote starts as: 'be' the change. After thinking it was a great idea, because I am, after all, an ideas person, I sat with that thought and wondered how the hell I was going to 'be' a change. It's all well and good to say it, but how do you 'be' it? And if I were to be good at the 'be'-ing part, what effect would that really have? On. The. World?

What else was I to do but run a little mind scenario.

Stage left. In walks me, wanting to give up drinking alcohol. I could say it was lowering my vibe, because it was, and I think you might agree that it's uncool to have a low vibe. But, for the sake of social acceptance and to make this scenario flow a little better, I will say it was giving me a headache and I was losing my Sundays over it. Not how I wanted to spend my precious day off.

So, in invoking my change theory, I envisaged myself at a party with all my friends. I frock up. Sparkles on. Party ready. Guests are shouting to each other over the top of the music, regaling fabricated stories of grandeur and/or gossip. They're creating a new reality, plied with alcohol. There's a lot of bluffing and blustering. I'm there. Joining in with my sparkling mineral water. Yes, I'm telling everyone it's Vodka because people freak out if you're not going to get as drunk as they are. If you have control of yourself, if you remain sensible, I quickly learned you're 'on the outta'.

My answer was there.

I could not be the change unless I was totally at one with my mineral water-drinking ways. I couldn't fake it to hope my world changed around me. I had to accept all aspects of me, including the one that needed to be accepted by others, before that could realistically happen. Then, I thought, *how does my not drinking, publicly, do anything at all but get me unfriended?* The thought of being ostracised, like an ostrich,[39] didn't really appeal to me, particularly as I don't like putting my head in the sand.[40] On that note, I decided, for now, that I wouldn't pursue that manner of world changing. I guess I didn't understand the underlying meaning of that quote.

---

39 *Yes, I did look those words up to see if they were related, but sadly, they are not. I'm just saving you the trouble.*

40 *Or other bodily parts for that matter. Trust me on this. In one of my beach yoga classes, the wind whipped up and gave us all a good exfoliation. My students reported back that sand was making its presence known in the most unusual of places for days afterward.*

I more recently discovered, however, that Gandhi's quote was merely a bumper sticker version of these beautiful words:

> "We but mirror the world. All the tendencies present in the outer world are to be found in the world of our body. If we could change ourselves, the tendencies in the world would also change. As a man changes his own nature, so does the attitude of the world change towards him. This is the divine mystery supreme. A wonderful thing it is and the source of our happiness. We need not wait to see what others do."

With that kind of encouragement, I decided to 'out' my mineral water-drinking ways with offering real substantiation for my choices. Secretly, some people told me they wished they could do the same thing.

After training in and studying the capabilities of the subconscious mind more deeply, Gandhi's quote suddenly made a great deal more sense to me. I was to somehow find within myself the ability to completely let go of the need for external acceptance. Accepting myself at a core level allowed me to stand in my own space. From comments made to me, I believe my stance has indeed reflected in others at a certain level.

Our lives as small and innocent children depended on the adults around us for our survival. In our small minds, the only power we held to ensure that survival was by doing things to keep the adults happy with us. Recall that approval, to our small selves, meant we were acceptable and lovable. We would be fed, clothed and sheltered. At that age, being loved equated to survival. This understanding really is fundamentally powerful stuff.

It was no wonder then, that if our actions in our child minds were disapproved of by the adults, which in turn threatened our lovable status, we learned very quickly to not repeat an action. There arose a threat. Within ourselves. Internal conflict. To our naïve little minds, that part of us causing the trouble was best tucked neatly away. Wrapped up in an unacceptability blanket, never to see the light of day again.

We treated part of our very own self as unacceptable. We hid it away. We became resistant to aspects of ourselves at the behest of others. We started formulating beliefs that were essentially untrue. Like, it's not okay to cry. Or, you shouldn't feel jealous of your big sister's new doll. Those feelings and emotions ARE, in fact, okay. More than that, at that age you needed to express those emotions. That's how you experienced the world. You were too young to rationalise life or to gain experiences any other way.

That inability to express ourselves meant we could no longer trust ourselves and as a result our relationship with ourselves was in danger. This is important to realise. That a conflict now exists. You are in the conflict with yourself. This continues into your grown-up world where you couldn't tell them it's not Vodka in your mineral water so as to be accepted. To be loved. To survive in this world.

You are now the 'I' in the conflict.

It is not a natural state of being to live with internal conflict. People avoid conflict in all sorts of ways. As lawyers we see a client's conflict being handed to us on a platter. If they pay us enough money, the problem then seems to become our very own to solve. Some people throw hate at it, thinking that hate + more hate = peaceful solution. Interesting equation. Some try to hide from it by numbing it in escapist ways. Yes, some of these can be fun, but they're not sustainable.

The kind folk in these examples have forgotten that without the participation of their good selves, their conflict would not exist. There is no running, numbing or paying someone else to fix it. It is enmeshed within them, and it remains for the individual to dive right in and greet it head on. There is no hide, only seek in this game.

By looking for the dissociated aspect of yourself within your inner world, you can locate and unravel from the safety blanket of unacceptability, a part of you that you previously found unacceptable. The point is, that dissociated part was always a real and valid part of you. It still is. The sad part. The angry part. The part that thought it was unlovable. The fun part. Yes, whilst these aspects may usually be described as having a more negative slant, some disowned parts can even be positive.

At the time, we thought those parts were best buried never again to see light of day. Some have even referred to these missing parts as wounds arising from the trauma we've experienced. We are hurt, and we need to be able to heal that hurt. Once we can shine a light on these very valid parts of us and see that we are allowed to be sad, we are allowed to be angry; we are allowed to be stupid or silly and have fun, we no longer have to hide our truest selves. We were right at the time to *FEEL* the way we felt, despite any disapproval.

Bringing to light the part of you that felt shame, for instance, whilst hard to feel right now, will heal many aspects of yourself. I have looked. I have found many of my missing bits. No doubt I have many more to find. But in doing so, I see the vista of this world like I'm sitting from a mountain top rather than from the muddy depths of despair. And the view, I must say, is pretty good from here. The only way is up. After moving on 'in', of course.

I've used what I'd learned from self-study, in my trainings, and from working with others. I had seen how bringing a shadow to awareness totally changes a person's perspective on their life.

Someone may, for instance, have an unnatural fear of birds. The majority of us think birds are just birds, yet you find that person was attacked by a bird when they were young and didn't deal with that trauma. It could have been a scenario where as a child, they were constantly left alone with the pet parrot for company. Their carer didn't protect them against the parrot's idea of a pecking order. That trauma then remains with them until it's looked at. Once the person can understand how they could have realistically been justified in feeling that birds could have looked like scary creatures to them, they are able to process the trauma. They are then able to see birds from a different perspective.

The ability to view the world from another point of view, with different glasses on so to speak, is wonderful. Working with your shadow will offer you this opportunity every time. It will enable you to see that what seems wrong in your life is not so wrong after all. In fact, there is rightness in how your shadow came to be, because you were the one who, unconsciously, tucked away that aspect of your own life.

This was beneficial to you at the time and so you need to be congratulated for taking these self-preserving steps. As an adult it is time to investigate whether or not those beliefs still hold the same validity for you.

Shining a light – revealing your perfection

The difficulty is, humans are complex. We are blind to our own perspective. We cannot see what we don't know exists within us. For this, we do need to take a look at the physical world around us for the clues.

In looking for our green pencil, it is likely that many situations will arise in your life providing you with opportunities to find it. You might, for instance, notice that people closest to you are wearing green. But that green for some reason upsets you and you want it to disappear. Everyone else is parading around in it and it's agitating you. You wish all these people would just come to their senses and choose another colour to wear, like sunny yellow. You rationalise that it's their fault you're unhappy with all their green-wearing.

The reality is, deep down you had suppressed your green-with-envy. The green showing up in your life was just mirroring what was going on within you. You had no idea until you were able to see what was going on around you – in your physical reality – was just a reflection of what was going on within. You had suppressed the jealousy you had over your big sister's doll. You were told it wasn't nice to be jealous and to want things for yourself. But in actual fact, it was okay for you to feel that way.

Once you recognise it, by bringing it into your awareness and then validating it, the green with envy will form part of your perfect self as you are no longer concealing it as a subconsciously lower energy. You are allowed to feel jealous. It is part of your spectrum of emotions. By suppressing that feeling, and not allowing it to flow through like energy should, it got stuck. It got stuck within your energy field and resonated on a lower frequency. By recognising it, and in doing so freeing the stuck energy, you will no longer be a match to the lower vibration of jealousy and the good green-flaunting folk, the one's 'making' you jealous will disappear from your external world. In doing this, as Ram Dass says, you are 'polishing the mirror'.

What a relief to know that it is your good self that has the power to change your whole world. It is within you. I had never heard better news. I have seen this work for me and others. In my teens, on more than one occasion, I had older people say to me they noticed I had a serious look on my face. As a teenager, I thought they were quite mad. I wasn't at all serious in my teen mind. It wasn't until later in life, I realised I was absolutely serious. I was the exact opposite of fun. Silliness was just so silly. Embarrassing even. Well, you can guess what that shadow was about? I'd lost my unacceptable silly somewhere on the track to adulthood, but rest-assured, I've found that silly shadow and sewed it firmly back on. My silly is intact, and right where it belongs, if you hadn't already noticed.

By merely recognising their existence, you can correct those subconscious beliefs and misconceptions, and *you* take on an entirely different perspective.

This is miraculous business.

I've seen some people even change their perspective before my eyes. The relief overcomes them with the understanding and acceptance of who they truly are. Those who thought they should feel guilty in a situation no longer feel the guilt. Those who have felt lonely, understood they had been abandoned either physically or emotionally as infants. They learned they were right to feel the way they felt. For instance, they understood that they were allowed to feel the sadness and the fear of complete abandonment rather than to have to 'suck it up' and be brave. That those feelings of sadness and fear belong to them, without judgement. Those feelings were separated from them then, and they could just as easily be brought home and nurtured as part of their fullest self. They are able to acknowledge the emotion does in fact exist within them and they are no longer a magnet to others that need to show them this.

Based on that appealing notion of being the change you want to see in the world, I looked a little deeper. I wanted to see if the change these people felt in their lives translated to changes around them. After all, if you're no longer holding onto that guilt at a subconscious level, then you should no longer attract situations to encourage your guilt to bubble to the surface. That means the world should look different to you.

Whilst I enjoy my lurking dogs and chocolatey-coated rocket science analogies, I have had the privilege of working with many real people, some of whom have been able to report back on direct shifts in their relationships. Those relationships move from a position of powerlessness and separateness to understanding for themselves, and in turn a greater understanding for the plight of others. Some shifts happen relatively quickly, some take a little longer. However, it's all governed by accessibility to the subconscious mind.[41]

Finding our shadows and shining a light on them effectively removes their existence. You must express emotions that you have tucked away, else they can even manifest in the physical body as pain and other dis-ease.[i] Yes, that's the way I like to refer to disease. In that you are not at ease with yourself.

Here's where I brave the pages and expose some of my very own dark places. I'll keep it short and sweet, the latter of which I assure you is the best word, because locating shadows is the sweetest business out there.

Anger

All my life I had suffered from back pain, well, from as young as I can remember anyway. My concerned mother sought all kinds of remedies when I was young. As I got older, I continued her work and took myself off to see chiropractors, underwent myotherapy, acupuncture, meridian healing, reiki, massage... oh dear, the list must stop there. I would gain some relief from these therapies, but the pain would return. Over the last couple of years, I was beginning to understand why no-one could find anything seriously enough wrong with me to warrant persistent pain. Dismissing this initially as utter nonsense, I continued with my round-robin therapy approach. Pain relief. Pain return. Rinse. Repeat.

During this period, I 'accidentally' purchased a book by Dr John Sarno, MD entitled *Healing Back Pain, The Mind-Body Connection*. I placed that book neatly on my 'to be read' pile. It's a large pile.

---

41 *In some instances, the ego will cause resistance as it protects its identity. There are ways of managing this, which are beyond the scope of this book.*

The book ended up buried near the bottom in the ensuing months after many other 'accidental' book purchases. Books are like shoes to me – delicious.

Anyway, I was at a point where the pain was driving me crazy. I consulted one of my favourite energy healers. Yes, I believe in that stuff, and it's quite okay if you don't. She told me I was angry and that I should consult a particular book by Dr Sarno. I laughed so loud it nearly hurt more than the back pain. Me? Angry? Pftt!!!

Incidentally, did I mention I already had in my possession the book to which she had referred me? Even funnier, I discovered that I was an extremely angry person. Anger that never saw the light of day in the truest sense but was popping out in bodily pain and via other angry people showing up in the mirror of my life. This particular back pain disappeared immediately on this discovery and the angry people did too. Wow! When I say the angry people disappeared, what I mean is, no, people weren't suddenly all sparkles and unicorns, but my perspective of angry people weirdly changed. I just didn't get as upset by other people's anger. It had way less of an effect on me. I was able to really see the person behind the anger. Not just the anger itself. This was such a revelation to me.

I'm still not brilliant at processing my own anger, it's a work in progress. The important thing is, anytime I recognise the signs that I'm holding on to it, I say a fat thank you to those signs and take a good look at why I'm resistant to processing it. Sometimes it's far from obvious. Because I was not outwardly angry I didn't think that emotion was something within me. I was right. It seems I had this strange idea that angry was not a cool emotion to exhibit. Go figure.[42] Now I know it must be expressed to be an effective e-motion. It sets my boundaries. Anger is also one of those cover emotions for feelings like fear, powerlessness or victimhood,

---

42 *Sarcasm doesn't translate easily to book pages.*

for instance. Which leads me to tell you what I uncovered after processing my anger. The deeper shadow.

Victimisation and powerlessness

I, like many other innocent children, was subjected to chronic childhood sexual abuse.[43] From what I allow myself to remember, the abuse endured for around 10 years. I felt ugly and dirty. As a result I rationalised that no one could get close to a person who was 'ugly and dirty', so I was unable to maintain lasting friendships. As I matured, I felt that this abuse had ruined my life. I was afraid of complete intimacy. With anyone. I felt shame and solitude. I gained weight to *prove* my ugliness and to protect me against closeness. And then I developed addictions to numb the pain of the resulting loneliness

As is the general profile in cases like mine, I was manipulated due to an imbalance of power by a person who effectively held a position of trust. The fact of the matter being, as a child, I was powerless to do anything to prevent what was happening to me. I felt victimised and unloved as no-one rescued me from what I grew to feel was an obvious injustice. There are many ways people will respond to abuse. For me, one response was to become a person that let others make the choices for me. I gave away my personal power. I acted like a doormat. A victim.

In chronic cases of abuse, you will find many shadows. There were many repressed aspects of myself to be found. Scary at first, but well worth the effort. Whilst I dealt with each one as they arose over time, ultimately, I sat with the realisation that my power was taken from me. My power of choice. My power of prevention. My power of anger. My power of anything.

---

43 *That was hard to write on paper. For everyone to see.*

My repressed anger was a cover emotion for being victimised. My inability to express it meant I was unable to set boundaries and so formed my inner victim. In holding onto my victim mentality, it at least meant I wasn't entirely powerless. I was one step up from the bottom rung. Choosing victimhood over powerlessness meant I had *some* power at least.

It broke my heart to see my childhood self at the mercy of such exploitation. But, I can find the beauty in my subsequent ability to 'rescue' her from those memories and to regain the power I had lost. I integrated those shadows. I no longer find myself in situations where I'm powerless to express myself when others endeavour to manipulate me or exert control over my life. My boundaries are now firmly in place.

I want to wander off for a short moment and posit that underneath all of our shadows is the feeling of powerlessness. How we deal with it rising from that low place is just a matter of degree. This idea makes sense to me, given that our carers were the ones holding the positions of ultimate power. It is a result of their disapproval of certain actions of ours, that we lost our power of choice. The choice to feel exactly how we wanted to feel. To act out the way we felt like acting out at the time. As we moved into adulthood, it was so necessary for us to reclaim our ability to exercise that power. The power of choice. Free will. This allows us the ultimate freedom to be who we truly are. Grand creators. I feel there are many of us right now, living our day-to-day lives under the power of someone else. Being what someone else wants us to be. There is so much more I learned from these life experiences, which I will be better positioned to share when the time is right.

Working with our shadow aspect not only has benefits for us in an individual space, it goes further. As lawyers, we could not possibly understand what abandonment would feel like in our clients if we have not acknowledged loneliness for ourselves.

Any method or combination of methods for exposing our shadows can be effective. I've tried differing methods under the most testing of conditions with a variety of people. That's for another book, I think. Most importantly, it's in reaching the awareness that there are aspects of ourselves we repressed during our childhood. We need to dig them out and bring them home to us so that we can view this life with a full spectrum of emotions in our toolkit. It's here we find the green pencil and pop it neatly back into the empty space in the pencil box.

In healing your traumas, in turn, the 'I' within your inner conflict is resolved and is then reflected in our personal reality. We are now equipped to see the world from a new perspective.

Again, I need to reiterate that we just can't go all out blaming our parents for our shadow debacle. Suffice to say, that their parents had a hand in their behaviour as their parents' parents did to them, and so on. It's an ancestral thing. It doesn't end looking back. But looking to the future, it could end with you. In fact, again I say, we should be thanking them. If we can see into our traumas, it's a little self-realisation that's going on for us. That is one of the greatest treats you can bestow upon yourself. On this point, I was interested in the viewpoint of Alan Watts, who observed:

> *"It may be necessary to divide the child against itself for the purpose of learning certain patterns of social behavior, but if the child does not later in life discover that this division was, like the myth of Santa Claus, a trick, it turns into a permanently alienated personality."*[m]

Food for thought. I lean toward this way of thinking, it supports my views in Part II, that we are having this human experience to learn and expand our consciousness. To grow as humans and, in turn, build strength in team humanity. What may seem really unfair could just be the best thing happening to you. That is how I view my life experiences. And this is how I view my clients as they sit before me with their world falling apart. On that note, it would be great to have people relate to the words of Thaddeus Golas: "*When you learn to love hell, you will be in heaven*".

It does take the courage to step into your own space and really look at what's happening, but as I've experienced, once you deal with your shadows, your outlook on the world changes. Imagine if I was still living in the victim mentality. I certainly would not be telling you this. I would be too afraid of exposing myself to criticism. I now stand in my own power. Life is no longer out to control how I live it. Yes, I am angry that my life could have been a little more on the sparkly side, but in my ability to now mostly express that anger, I am also able to better establish my personal boundaries. I now live, for the most part, as open and true to me as I can be at this point in my life.

I'm in support of Jung's utilitarian words: "*We cannot change anything until we accept it*". Bring your shadow out, as that delicious forgotten part of you, and you can change your entire view on life. On embracing and assimilating your own shadows, at the very least, you will begin to liberate yourself from believing that the world is out to get you. You will see that it really is all about you. I reiterate, the idea that the shadow exists in the first place is because it's central to our growth.

Putting the 'fun' in your fundamentals, we can see that which bothers us most is nestled neatly as gems within the conflicts surrounding us. Once we have a handle on ourselves, we can do the same for others. Lawyers particularly have more opportunity to advance humankind from this setting.

The sad part for we lawyers is that we are trained to focus on people's problems as being external to them. We gather evidence and show them: "*look, it's not your fault, it says it right here on the judgment*". If we don't assist a client to move their minds inward, that person you just extricated from one legal tangle will get themselves right into another one. And what's frustrating is, it will smack very similarly of the last debacle they found themselves in. Why do you think we have recidivism?

However, before we can effectively work with others, we need to work with ourselves. Not only so we can see how this works for us in the most positive sense of our being, but to see how viewing life from this perspective anchors us to human connection at a core level.

By the way, in case your shadows have now led you to believe there is something wrong with you, there is not. All that's happened is you have protected yourself. You did the right thing for you, in keeping yourself safe at the time. That safety mechanism is now merely operating as a background program. And a fine program it's been. Now that you're all grown up and no longer rely on your carers for your survival, you can exercise your ability to choose. That means you can choose to see that these programs are no longer required in your latest operating system. A little defragmentation of that internal hard drive of yours is all that's required.

If you want to change how your day job pans out, as you have seen, it all starts within you. You have probably realised that you can run, but you can't hide from the internal you. That might be motivation enough to set some polishing in motion. You can then check your look in the mirror to see how that internal change is panning out for you. Check out those around you. Say to yourself, how am I looking today? If someone gets you all crossed-up, thank them. That's right. You heard it here first. Thank that person for the great gift they just offered you by showing you your shadow. Then get to work on it. The power is with you only. The choice to collect your gifts is all yours.

As I move on, you will see why you might like to exercise this choice sooner rather than later.

CHAPTER

4

Feelings, nothing more than feelings

In the last three chapters we considered a few important things:

1. People have a right brain that connects with feelings. Lawyers are people. Therefore, lawyers too, have feelings.

2. Feelings must be felt, or they'll bite you when you least expect it.

3. You can look in your world mirror to find the feelings that you tucked away.

My brilliant skills of deduction therefore, tell me that this is really all about feelings. I have shown you that contrary to public opinion on the question of whether lawyers have feelings, they are, in fact, in there. Some of them ready for the unpacking, some of them in hiding still.

First, you might like to know how feelings come into existence. What, in fact, is their *modus operandi*? Yes, I think all of us agree that you can move your person in a way that can physically feel things – hot, cold, soft, prickly. But how do you get to feel prickly in its emotional form? How indeed does this happen from a neuroscientific standpoint?

Again, Dr Joe has the answers. He has observed that:

> "When you think a thought (or have a memory), a biochemical reaction begins in your brain causing the brain to release certain chemical signals. That's how immaterial thoughts literally become matter—they become chemical messengers. These chemical signals make your body feel exactly the way you were just thinking. Once you notice you are feeling a particular way, then you generate more thoughts equal to how you're feeling, and then you release more chemicals from your brain to make you feel the way you've been thinking. The next thing you know, you get caught in a loop where your thinking creates feeling and your feeling creates thinking."[m]

This is powerful information. You think a thought. Your body translates that thought into a feeling. Your brain then says *"ooh, look, I'm feeling a feeling"* and then that, being a thought, registers a feeling, and around we go again. A thought/feeling loop.

You see something that rubs you up the wrong way. You think angry thoughts. Your body gets prickly. Your mind registers your prickly feeling and says, *"Oh yes! She's angry."* Your thought validates your angry prickle. Your logical brain says, *"I feel prickly, therefore I am angry"*. My body happily accepts that as my present state of being. And around we go again. Now you understand why it is so hard to get some thoughts out of your head. It's a merry-go-round. Mostly, without the 'merry'.

Thought-loops. They're loopy! E-motion. Energy in motion. They are mostly of the negative variety and that's because of our all-powerful subconscious mind. Recollect that negative energy when stored in the subconscious is mighty powerful. As a result, we love to sway to the negative side of the ledger as a justifiable state of being (in our minds) when we have shadow aspects of ourselves skulking below the conscious surface. That's why it seems far easier to believe that bad things are happening to us as opposed to the good things.

That said, this is why I love to remind myself of my favourite Taoist proverb[44], which opens our minds to the possibility that some things that seem bad at the time, might just turn out for the best. It's just like the 'every cloud has a silver lining' thing. If it's a shadow aspect you're looking at, it's not in fact a bad thing. I say it's a good thing, provided you're ready to roll up your sleeves and start dealing with it.

It follows that remaining trapped on a downer of a thought-loop is not the healthiest way to live our lives. In discussing the causes of cardio-vascular and most other diseases, Dr Lipton has discovered they are primarily lifestyle related, and can be influenced by our change in perception. His studies have revealed:

> *"The brain secretes blood-borne hormones, stress factors, and inflammatory agents in order to coordinate the function of 50 trillion cells to sustain life ... [and that] ... the cell membrane is the information processor that provides the interface between biology and our brain's perception of the environment."*[b]

If you are in stress mode, so are your cells. It would seem obvious then, that we must decipher a way to get off the that thought merry-go-round. You subscribed to this loop by your way of

---

44 To illustrate the notion that you usually cannot tell for certain whether something is either good or bad, I've been wanting a spot to recite my favourite Taoist proverb. "This is a story of a farmer whose horse ran away. That evening the neighbours gathered to commiserate with him since this was such bad luck. He said, 'May be.' The next day the horse returned, but brought with it six wild horses, and the neighbors came exclaiming at his good fortune. He said, 'May be.' And then, the following day, his son tried to saddle and ride one of the wild horses, was thrown, and broke his leg. Again the neighbors came to offer their sympathy for the misfortune. He said, 'May be.' The day after that, conscription officers came to the village to seize young men for the army, but because of the broken leg the farmer's son was rejected. When the neighbors came in to say how fortunately everything had turned out, he said, 'May be.'"

Shortened interpretation by Watts, Alan. Tao: The Watercourse Way (Kindle Locations 675-681). Souvenir Press. Kindle Edition.

thinking and it will keep sending messages to your 50 trillion cells which sync with your brain until you opt out.

Opt out of the downer and opt out of dis-ease.

As Dr Lipton has discovered, when we change the way we identify with the world, that is, when we 'change our beliefs', we change the blood's neurochemical composition, which then initiates a complementary change in the body's cells.[p] Seems to me like a good plan. Happy cells, happy life. That one's reciprocal and reversible.

Dr Joe has discovered that this *"thinking-feeling loop also produces a measurable electromagnetic field that surrounds our physical bodies.[q] The only way we can change our lives is to change our energy—to change the electromagnetic field we are constantly broadcasting."*[r]

You knew you had a magnetic personality, now you know it's not just magnetic, it's *electro*magnetic. That's far more exotic. I'm full of good news!

As Dr Joe explains, the electromagnetic field arising from our thought-feeling loops that are surrounding us, can be palpably felt by others. Like in the tuning fork example I provided earlier, you can tune into another's vibe. You certainly can feel the subtly different vibes in say, coming into your toddler's room when they're just innocently playing, compared to when they're 'innocently playing' whilst trying to ensure you avoid noticing the 'art' they created on the wall with the Vegemite from their sandwich. No words need be exchanged, you tune in easily to these subtle but distinctly different vibes. One is based in love. One in fear.

You might be familiar with say, going into a pre-litigation mediation. Yes, the idea of that meeting is to resolve the conflict without taking the matter to litigation. Funnily enough though, the initial feeling when you walk into one of these meetings is more often than not an icy environment. You can feel the opposition to your just being in that room. Right to the very core of you.

In the meeting, there is the feeling of 'us' and 'them'. You can feel separation. This is fear-based. You are concerned there will be attacks on you, so you also put up shields of defence. A subtle war-like environment is present, despite the intention that the parties need to get together to resolve the issue. How can such an environment be conducive to effective resolution when all we feel is separation?

It is easy to see over time how that scenario becomes a hard-wired thought-feeling loop. This would manifest in all the lawyers going into that room having that dreaded preconceived thought, which feeds the fear vibe, which feeds the thought. It's now a program within you and everyone else in the mediation that's running. Result: icy, fearful environment.

To unsubscribe to the negative 'thought-mail' your body is receiving, to hop off the merry-go-round at the fun stop, you need to make a real effort to change your thoughts first. This is what Dr Joe means when he says, change your energy. Recall that thoughts are energy. It follows then that we need to train our minds to look at life differently. Our mind is our brain in action.[5] So we need to revisit our thought processes and learn how to train that dragon. To stop it from reacting with fire when we'd rather it didn't.

Therefore, to become kissable, it's highly probable that we need to think the type of thoughts that will make us feel kissable. We must imagine ourselves as being the person who is so kissable that the mere thought of being kissed sends tingles into our body, which makes us feel kissable and gets us more kisses. I think I've just discovered pure perpetual kissable e-motion right there. Think warmer, fuzzier thoughts and they will translate to a warmer, fuzzier body. Then we'll all look like teddy bears and live happily ever after *sigh*. It's all in how we think.

How then do we keep our fuzzy on when we're in the middle of our day jobs and things are going pear-shaped before our very eyes? Or, even, can we? I've seen many colleagues move away from the practise of law once they experienced those elusive warm and fuzzy feelings in their lives. Fair enough. Legal practise seems to act like a razor that shaves the fuzzy right off! I want us to be able to practise law and still feel awesome. Like what we are doing has real meaning to people, that everyone we encounter in our practice will walk away feeling better for the experience. Fuzziness all round. That thought makes me feel warm and fuzzy for sure.

Let's contemplate for a moment, how this could be achieved. You are training that dragon. That trusty and sometimes fire-breathing left brain of yours. It's softening, allowing the right brain some touchy-feely air time. You just know you're doing great. You get all your ducks in a row. You're the poster child of positive intention. Positivity is poppin' out of you everywhere. You've got sticky notes announcing 'I am successful' all over the refrigerator. You've fashioned your dog into a moving vision board. You have a reminder set on your phone displaying hourly aides-memoire that you love you. You sit Pollyanna-style with your friends at lunch, saying "Wow, that's great!", being confident that your force field of sparkles and unicorns will fend off any negativity threatening to sully your high vibes.

Then out of no-where, one of your lunch chums informs you that your so-called best friend went behind your back, applied for, and *got* the promotion you told her you had your heart set on. Sparkles fall to the floor. Unicorn horn deflates. You feel physically crushed. On the spot.

You now sit there and wonder in disbelief where all those positive thoughts got you now? No best friend. No promotion. You had the vision board. On the dog, no less.

Once again, I'm going to poop the party. If we wonder why we can't change it all despite all our positive thinking, it comes right back to the self-limiting beliefs you are subconsciously holding onto. Remember, a belief is just a thought. So those all-powerful subconscious beliefs will form thought-loops just the same as conscious thoughts and beliefs do.

I'll give you an example once dear to my heart. Summer's coming and you want to lose weight. You've just landed upon the lemon crunchy granola diet, which promises to be a 'sure thing'. Of course, you saw the failings of your previously road-tested peach and watermelon detox diet, too many colours. You set out faithfully following the diet plan. The first few days show you evidence of success. You will be bikini (or man-kini as the case may be) ready in just weeks! Two weeks in, you are positively starving. You are irritable. You really never want to see a lemon or a granola. Ever. Again. You weaken at the next office birthday party and have just a small slice of Martha's famous chocolate torte with lemon-swirl icing. It has lemon on it so it must be ok, you rationalise. Then all hell's broken loose as guilt sets in.

You reprimand yourself for that silly mistake, mentally chastise that traitor chocolate for being so tempting and to make yourself FEEL better you get home lusting after chocolate and polish off two whole blocks of [*insert favourite chocolate here*]. Do you see how diets do not work for you? The real reason you are not losing weight is because there is a subconscious belief you are holding onto that the weight you are carrying is keeping you safe somehow. This is evidenced by the feelings you had whilst you were on the diet. You were conflicted. You wanted to stay on the Impossible Diet Plan, but chocolate was waging an all-persuasive internal subconscious war in your mind. And it was winning. The moment you tucked into the chocolate you were comforted. You felt filled up. You felt safe.

We saw the effects of internal conflict in the last chapter. Internal conflict not only shows up as triggers in your life directing you to find some shadows wanting your attention, it also has the bonus of showing you that something is 'off' with your chosen direction in life. You are not able to truly tune into with what FEELS right. You are doing all the right things imagining yourself in that bikini and feeling good about it. You are trying to create a new thought-loop. However, there are feelings that were formed from solid subconscious thought-loops you hard-wired into your programming a *long* time ago. This is another way our comrade the human shadow shows up in action.

Until you can recognise this, you remain trapped in your old thought paradigm. The good people in the weight-loss industry bank on you not knowing this. I know I'm side tracking, but again, I stand as human evidence that dealing with the shadow helped me no end to maintain a sensible weight all the while making chocolate my friend and not the enemy, despite my disparaging remarks in this book about said friend.

This is not just about diets. It's about all life situations where you believe you need to change, but something thwarts the process. Other classic examples include, "I would love to win the lottery, all my life's problems will be solved". Or, where you've found a new life partner and "Yay! I've found the love of my life, I will live happily ever after". In the lotto example, how many people have you seen win squillions of dollars to become more destitute post lotto win than before.

Additionally, and I have seen this as a family lawyer, there are many people who leave their current partner to find a new 'love of their life' to end up in the same mess as the last time. I am expanding on the vibe discussion in the previous chapter. These are just your subconscious feelings at work. Those created from your past experiences. Once you deal with the self-limiting beliefs you hold, you can begin to create new beliefs that, based on better thoughts will, in turn, create new supporting feelings.

This again is showing you that buying that shiny new Porsche – which, do not misunderstand me, is a lovely thing to own if you want it simply for the sake of appreciation; however, if you want it because you think having it will make you feel better, then you are seeking your happiness in an inverted kind of way. You are trying to fill the space where a missing feeling should be. And that, as we've seen in my lemon crunchy granola diet, does not work. Rather than offer ourselves transient treats, we need to look for the transcendent treats that make effective moves in the direction toward achieving our highest kissability quotient.

Whilst filling up with fun things helps us feel great in the short term, we need to really look into our pasts before we can move forward into sustaining that feel-good vibe. When we can create more satisfying thought-loops, we find there is less internal conflict and as a result, greater internal satisfaction. You will therefore buy the Porsche for all the right reasons and feel gratified.

I'm now going to explain why you need to feel the feelings you've tucked away. First and foremost, your feelings form part of who you are. They are in your body. Good feelings help you feel light and airy. Not so good feelings do the opposite. They show you that you are heavy and dragging something unwanted around with you. This is what's called the mind-body connection. In any event, they're called feelings because you're supposed to *feel* them. All of them. We have now seen that thoughts and feelings are a team. They work together to make your day better, or not.

You now know that the thoughts and feelings you formed in the past, based on your life's experiences, dictate how you see the world today. They can really affect your decision making. You might go into a store for instance and gravitate more toward the sales person who looks honest to you. Why is that? Perhaps it's the colour of their shirt you trust or the smell of their perfume. All things are based in your memories, because you've allowed your past to have control of your future.

Those memories you have come complete with feelings. They are very real and need to be treated with respect. The good student that you are has already grasped the notion that if you try to tuck them away to play another day, they don't listen. They'll come out to play when they want and at the most inappropriate time. And they don't play nice. They are cross with you for hiding them because they are of the opinion that you are being no fun at all when you do so.

Then, what else are feelings good for other than their annoying games of hide and seek?

Connecting the humans

Have you ever watched one of those 'silly' television show where daredevils, usually of the late teen male variety, are filmed falling off skateboards as a result of their lack of 'thinking it through' skillset? You watch on, hands partially covering your eyes, knowing that you don't really want to, but are strangely compelled to see what's coming next. Invariably something unfortunate happens to them. You feel their pain, right? You start by thinking "*Ow, that's gotta hurt!*", and right away you feel it. Thoughts, as we've learned, are an integral part to the feeling process. You know what it's like to fall over and physically hurt yourself. We've done it. We've felt it. We are all connected in that way. Usually from our experiences. We have the ability to think of a memory and feel what it was like to fall off our own bike.

A memory brings with it real feelings. As do all thoughts, past and future.

Like in the bike example, you need to experience a feeling before you can understand how that feels in another. It's the idea that we are all separate and not connected in any way that's the central drawback to human understanding. It took Jill Bolte Taylor to have a stroke to learn that our right brain sees us as being connected. To everything. But I'm sure you don't want to take it that far to understand this concept. If you liked my sealed section, you will get my more left-of-field perspective on oneness. Again, it's all about energy. Even if you find that hard to believe, you will no doubt agree that you still feel it when someone's 'in your space'. Whilst you can't see the physicality of it, you can feel a connection.

An analogy of oneness in action is this. Say you start the day by treating yourself to a coffee at that new café down the road. The dude making your coffee ignores your good morning smile in his 'too cool for hipster school' attitude. Your eyebrows raise at his indifference and you feel flat. You head to the office with your less than hip coffee in relation to its fancy eco-organically-moonlit-grown-sourced-under-the-morning-dew-of-the-equinox-quantum-leaf price tag. No-one notices your new haircut. You feel worse. Does my hair look bad, you wonder. The deadline for filing Very Important Court Document passed yesterday. Your PA 'forgot' to tell you but is conveniently letting you know over your now going cold yada yada coffee.

You try calling your opponent, knowing said opponent won't take your call due to 'surfing' commitments. You look out the window, noting the gentle off-shore breeze and do acknowledge the potential for catching a good wave. You wish you were out there too. Back to reality, you are freaking out. You are short with your assistant as you bark orders and between the lines she reads your surreptitious accusation: *"this is really your fault."* She is miffed at the covert dressing-down, and her day goes further downhill from there. She gets home, relieved to be away from the drama. Her partner doesn't listen to her day. In mindless frustration, she trips over the dog. The dog is annoyed. The dog, who does not have the memory of a goldfish, the next day takes his frustration out on the postie. Some scary bark barks later, the postie falls off her bike. She gets home that night in pain. Her kids want to go to the beach as the weather is equally as awesome as the day before, but she can't take them as she has a suspected broken foot. The kids take their frustration out on each other... I could go on.

There you have it. How my hipster barista's indifference affected the postie's kids' beach excursion is a nutshell example of connection. In six short degrees.

The point is, the concept of connectedness shows us that all conflicts affect more than just the people in the immediate vicinity. This thought-feeling loop we create in the form of a magnetic field transmits information to the space around us. It then continues its journey via the ripple effect. Your feelings truly connect with many others. In their minds and in their bodies and in more people than you may ever know.

The legal clients that come to see us have a legal problem, but they are not the problem.[45] I know that sounds obvious, but we tend to separate the person from the legal problem. They are, however, integral to it. It is their shadow that got them into this mess and shining the light on the shadow will help get them out of it. They are usually not in their best frame of mind because they are consumed by a problem they were unable to resolve on their own. In effect, they feel powerless. They rely on we lawyers to wield some power for them. My way of thinking suggests we should be empowering our clients to pick up that torch and shine some light on their darkness. We should not be taking charge on the chariot for them.

---

45 *Perhaps I've taken that one a bit far for some of you.*

"The tree which moves some to tears of joy is in the eyes of others only a green thing which stands in the way... As a man is, so he sees."[1]

William Blake's inspiring words reminded me that we need to be seeing our clients from the place that moves us to tears, in a good way! They are people in need of our empathy and connectedness. They are not mere objects in the way of our aspirations, they *are* our aspirations.

Ultimately, it is imperative for lawyers to be able to hold a compassionate space for clients. To understand what is really happening when a person is in conflict, and in the resulting powerless state in which they find themselves. Empathy is simply the ability to put ourselves in another's shoes to feel what they are feeling. But how can you possibly know and understand the full spectrum of someone else's feelings if you have been supressing your own feelings and emotions? How could you know the colour green if you had never seen it in all its rainbow-centred glory?

Obvious to me, is that we need to heal the relationship with ourselves. Bring ourselves back to feel the full spectrum of feelings so we can find our innate self and in turn smooth out our own inner conflicts. Diametrically opposed to conflict is harmony. Harmony and peace are friends. You need to be as close to being at peace with yourself as you can manage before you can even remotely try to objectively view the world from another's eyes.

I feel very strongly that because lawyers are the ones more likely to be exposed to relational conflict on a day-to-day basis, the greater the emphasis should be given to our skillset to create a safe, centred space from which to open to the needs of others. That may sound too touchy-feely for some, but as they say, you can't pour from an empty cup.

I'll pare it back a little. Recall in the case of *Brain v Brain,* learned Counsel for the Left put to the court that expressing emotions have been blamed as a weak trait to showcase. What wasn't reported in that case, was that Counsel went on to stress that breaking down in tears before the judge because you have *feelings* for the opposing client, was a most unsatisfactory state of affairs! Yes, I see where Left is coming from. But let me assure you, when you are truly in balance, such 'frightful displays' of humanity are quite acceptable.

Nonetheless, if you still can't trust that right hemisphere of yours, then know that it has backup. This one's a doozy.

Your heart's right where you left it

You may have heard others call you out on thinking with your heart and not your head. Well not you, specifically, you're a lawyer, I think we did establish earlier that the squishy thing formerly known as your heart was duly snuffed out under the burgeoning weight of that Suit of Armour. Sounds dramatic, but I think you'll agree there's an element of truth to my musings. That Suit has caused us separation. Separation from our hearts. The Suit of Separation... SOS.

Okay, so I've again segued right back to the heart. Don't look at me like that. It had to be done. Let's face it, you've no way of finding it, do you?

Our heart. Our soft, mallowy centre. The symbol of love. The first organ that forms during the development of the human embryo. The beautiful heart. It's the power house needed to carry nutrients and waste around the embryo to keep its cells alive via the circulatory system. It keeps us alive. It cares. It also attacks us when we don't look after it. It is a vital organ for more reasons than the obvious. It is at the centre of your being.

If letting go of staunch reliance on your left brain proves too much to bear, then let me pledge to you, hand on heart, that all is well. I'll let you in on another little discovery. Your heart has a mini brain. Aside from the real value it has in keeping you alive, its inherent intelligence will no doubt count as a valuable ally to lawyers.

A group known as the HeartMath Institute has undertaken over 25 years of scientific research on the psychophysiology of emotions and the interaction between the heart and brain. I'm tipping most of you had no idea that this pumping little fun packet of yours contains over 40,000 neurons, giving it the ability to sense, process information and help you make decisions. It produces the hormone oxytocin, aka the 'love' hormone and its very own electromagnetic field can also affect others around you. The heart has even demonstrated a type of learning and remembering function. And to top it off, it gives the brain more information than it receives. We're onto something here. It's better than a backup, it's a source and transmitter of sensory information. It's smarter than you think. Literally.

How amazing is all the clever blood pumping and dutifully nourishing capabilities that it undertakes – All. By. Itself. I dare you not to agree, it's miraculous.[46] And not only is it the only organ possessing innate intelligence (please, let's not shame our other cognitively-challenged organs), it also is feelings-oriented. You can be light-hearted. You can be heavy-hearted. You can even get all the way to broken-hearted. The full spectrum. Your heart can also feel full of love. For those of you who have children, I don't think your heart can get fuller than when you first see their crinkled little red faces enter this world.

---

46 *A short rant is needed here. The 'm' word is not something I use often, sounds too biblical. Childbirth too, is a miracle. Some seem to just accept that that's the way it all is, without delving deeper. They agree that no-one knows how it all works, but then close their minds, arms all crossed, to the options. I sincerely wish others could really zoom in on that miraculous component of we humans more often, it would open more minds to the question of who we really are.*

That last sentence is a clue to how your heart, despite all its intelligence, can also help you navigate this feelings business. When you are happy, full of hope and contentment, you can feel fulness in your heart. Like it's bursting with the plumpness of a fat feather pillow. On the other hand, when you feel stressed, you feel a tightness in your chest, it feels constricted. Maybe some of you have had your heart broken. Or experienced intense grief. You will feel that right in your heart. It's been emptied out. This is why you can't fill yourself up externally. Your heart will still feel empty if you allow the negative emotions to remain within you rather than allowing them to ultimately flow through.

These feelings your heart offers you, for free, are also great indicators of the choices you make in your life. Often, it's right within your heart that you can feel the answers to your own questions. If you can't come to terms with that concept just yet, all it takes is a little practise. Next time you are consciously choosing to do something of importance to you, first examine the feelings in your heart. If you are not sure of what you're feeling, just check in with the outcome of your choice. You'll soon get the hang of it. Your heart is never wrong. It's just the battle with your head, your ego mind, that you have to watch out for. That psycho!

Your heart is like a barometer for the emotions going on around you and within you. It rises to meet the sunny fine feelings in calm coherence, or it plummets with the onset of stormy drama, becoming spasmodic like lightning and thunder. The good people at the HeartMath Institute have put this in more technical terms confirming that:

> "During stress and negative emotions, when the heart rhythm pattern is erratic and disordered, the corresponding pattern of neural signals traveling from the heart to the brain inhibits higher cognitive functions. This limits our ability to think clearly, remember, learn, reason, and make effective decisions. (This

helps explain why we may often act impulsively and unwisely when we're under stress.) The heart's input to the brain during stressful or negative emotions also has a profound effect on the brain's emotional processes—actually serving to reinforce the emotional experience of stress.

In contrast, the more ordered and stable pattern of the heart's input to the brain during positive emotional states has the opposite effect–it facilitates cognitive function and reinforces positive feelings and emotional stability. This means that learning to generate increased heart rhythm coherence, by sustaining positive emotions, not only benefits the entire body, but also profoundly affects how we perceive, think, feel, and perform." [u]

Again, we see the loops. They occur in your heart too and send messages to your brain. This is why I like to take care of my peace centres during the day, so that my heart doesn't produce jaggedy lines or scribble. I don't want scribbly, jaggedy messages sent to my brain. Too messy.

You can quite sensibly apply this knowledge to your benefit when you appreciate that your heart is the one feeding the emotional energy to your brain. This is profound information for all of you who aspire to, at the very least, 'think clearly' in your day jobs. This is why it is important not only to move toward more positive thinking, but to live from the space in your heart. It's where the feelings are felt the best.

To get a visual on what your heart is trying to tell you, the HeartMath Institute has posted some helpful graphs on their website[v] showing the heart rhythm patterns during differing emotional states. The graph representing the state of your heart when stressed, angry or frustrated shows erratic jagged lines. This is your heart, people! That graph looks like your heart is having an attack! Frightening!

By contrast, the graph showing the heart under the more content emotions of appreciation, compassion or love, display lovely smooth wavy lines, representing heart coherence. What I found most interesting is that merely being in a passive state of relaxation does not necessarily equate with heart coherence, which is apparently only available to us when expressing the emotions of appreciation.[w]

I appreciate that

Appreciation. It is fundamental to finding the inner peace we so need. The gentle wavy lines on the HeartMath graph said so.[47] Appreciation and happiness are team members in connecting to inner peace. You won't find one without the other. You may rightly wonder how you can sit in appreciation of someone's attack on you. Or, even wonder how it is that you can appreciate the slow driver in the fast lane when you're late for work. Again, it's all a matter of perspective.

You really are the centre of the universe. Stuff is not happening 'to' you, it's happening 'for' you. To teach you many things, including appreciation. To achieve a pass, you are being handed gifts on a plate to work with. Start by studying your reaction to a drama you're facing. Then, if you're triggered, appreciate this as being a shadow brought to your attention whilst you note that you've got some polishing to do. If you're mildly annoyed, be mildly annoyed, angry even, feel those emotions, but for goodness sake, move them on. Don't hang onto them for more than about 90 seconds else you can come unstuck. More on the 90-second 'rule' as it's called, in the next chapter. Recognise that in the drama before you, there are *always* more factors at play than you will ever know. Moreover, you cannot control all the externals.

---

47 *As have many other inspiring individuals.*

Once you understand those few principles, you are ahead of the game.

In instances where you are at risk of a personal attack, where you have your inner self packaged neatly, with shadows enlightened, you will have no desire to attack a person if you find yourself in disagreement with them. Your intact self-worth can readily perceive the commonality and disparity of your views, respect them, and/or if necessary, offer up your own point of view.

However, if you are easily triggered, you will let fly at any perceived challenge to your self-worth. If you are the 'attackee' in this instance, then see yourself as being the gift to the dear soul with the loud and/or sarcastic tone. It's nothing at all to do with you at a personal level. Understand that your mere presence in this instance, exposes their shadow.

You can then sit in appreciation and understanding that the 'attacker's' shadow is playing out in public for all to see, and you can thank your good self for not buying in. Your heart will thank you for keeping it in a state of composure and you will be able to think more clearly. The 'attacker' will later sit in wonder at what happened as your higher energy did not meet with their lower energy. It's like you erected an impenetrable force field to the attack. All from your ability to appreciate what's really going on behind those dramatic scenes. Hopefully the 'attacker' later received some insight into unpackaging their own gift in the situation. Gifts all 'round, really!

Trust me, this works. It takes a little practise to hold your own space, but of the two of you, you're the one coming out the other end cultivating the healthier thought-feeling loops. Yes, it does positively affect your health, another reason to sit in appreciation.

Another instance in which many of us get antsy is when slow drivers hang out for longer than necessary in the fast lane.

Especially when you think that the things you have to do today are probably far more important than theirs. No, I know that 'you' don't think like that, but I've heard of people that do.

Can you believe it?

Anyway, for 'those' people, again, this is all a matter of perspective. There is no point in getting all messed up over things you can't control. You have no idea what that person in front of you is going through. They may have just received some shocking news and really don't even know what day it is. They may not realise you have very important things to do. They may not realise you are even behind them. For me, I usually imagine that I am being slowed down for a reason. Who knows, I may just have missed being involved an accident? You've gotta appreciate that!

Try to find the appreciation for any unpleasant situation you find yourself in. See things from all players' perspectives. Try and put yourself in their space for a moment. Whilst you have absolutely no idea what is really going on with them, it is beneficial to even appreciate the fact that you have no idea. No-one is out to attack you on purpose. Ever. You may find that one difficult to relate to, but once you truly understand the way a person sees the world is based on their own perceptions, it really is all about their way of thinking. Or your own. You may have now realised that when you have a problem with someone else, it really has nothing to do with them, per se. It's your subconscious belief that is creating the issue.

It really all comes down to you being able to appreciate these situations for being something other than what you may think they are. Again, always ask yourself: is this a good thing or a bad thing? I love that line. It opens your mind to the reality that you have absolutely no idea what will happen next. Appreciation for life's bumps in the road helps you move that emotional energy through you and settle back into a calm, coherent state of clarity and well-being.

Emotions affect your performance and your health with their looping effects. Whether that's bad or good, that again is a matter of perspective. If it seems like a bad thing, and your heart is getting all jagged, then you may need to question why that is. Are you getting triggered? Is there a shadow dulling your otherwise sunny day? If you recognise that, then the bad thing just became a good thing, then as Shakespeare's *Hamlet* noted: *"there is nothing either good or bad, but thinking makes it so"*. Let's make the choice to do that thinking with our hearts.

The heart connection

This is the missing 'peace' in the puzzle in our quest to become more kissable. I've taken a while to get here, but this is the heart of the matter. The heart connection. The full circle includes your mind, your body and your heart. You cannot favour one over the others else inner conflict arises. They are all parts of you and you need them to participate equally in your daily tasks.

We have seen that while most people live in their mind space, lawyers have been trained to carry out their day jobs there too. The intellectual mind is what we have been taught to use to analyse facts and build cases. We have firmed up neural pathways programming us to win our own client's case to the detriment of the other party despite, for the most part, there being valid standpoints of 'right' on each side.

This left-brain thinking succeeds in keeping us in a state of separation from one another. The Suit of Separation we've constructed over time has clouded our human connection. Through our hearts we can open those channels again.

I have imparted upon you the understanding that we, as energetic beings, share an indivisible connection. It is our natural state of being. It is our innate state. Trying to advance the world in separateness is, by its very nature, counterproductive. Capture some air in a jar. Put the lid on. It's still air in there. Like all the other air, its essence remains the same, it's now just separated in the jar and becomes stale. With humans, it's the same. The essence of connection remains; in separation that connectedness just manifests in outcomes with lower energies and emotions. The ultimate rippling outward then affects many other unsuspecting individuals in a negative fashion akin to my barista and the postie's children fable.

In order to live within our natural state, we need to shift the way in which we interact with others, and our feelings are our best indicators of whether we are shifting in the right direction. To change our current lawyer persona from the crush-kill-destroy model within the Suit of Separation, we are therefore going to have to inhabit a new way of being. That inhabitation is going to need to occur by first removing the Suit and shifting our vantage point to be at the heart level of the person behind the label called lawyer. There is a vast difference in how we can approach our lives based upon whether we are living solely in our heads or living more from our hearts.

Humans have needs. Needs that must be met. However, in satisfaction of those needs our left-brained, analytical, legal mind sees others as being separate. Our mind perceives others as merely being objects to satisfy our own desires. For instance, I need this client so I can win their case, garner a fine reputation as a litigator and earn serious money. This client is merely a means to my achieving that goal. When you are in this driven state you are usually operating from a place of fear. All the *"what if?"* questions are swimming around in the foundation of your mind. *"What if I'm not good enough?"*, *"What if I lose?"*, *"What will other's think of me?"* and so on. They are fear-based questions. The result is a closed heart connection.

The way this feels to those around you correlates with research conducted by Dr Joe, which says that our electromagnetic field, of which the heart has its very own, expands and contracts in direct response to our emotional state. When we are stressed we draw energy from our field of energy, we deplete it. You effectively starve yourself of energy and lose connection with those around you.

Look at your client as the whole person. Appreciate them. Consider first that in coming to see you they no doubt: a) don't really want to be seeing you at all, nothing personal of course; and b) don't want to be in the predicament they are in. You are seeing a real person with real feelings and real problems. When you approach your work from a state of appreciation, not only for yourself but for your client, you are coming from a heart-centred place. You have expanded your energy to include them. You are saying, "*my heart goes out to you*". You have truly connected with them.

It is only from this standpoint of appreciation that you can truly listen. You can hear who they are and what they are saying to you. In this space, your level of connection means both your needs are effectively being fulfilled. In separation, when living from the mind space, you are manipulating that person to fulfil your needs. In comparison to sitting with an open heart, manipulation sounds too much like hard work to me. From a place of appreciation, you can still represent the client. You can also appreciate the needs of all players in the game. You are expanded enough to see the big picture. You can see the ripple effects in meeting everyone's collective needs. Yes, you can still charge fees for your services, but you can do it from a connected place that delivers real satisfaction to best meet the needs of all.

I understand it takes willingness to allow vulnerability back into your life if you are to genuinely be able to settle into this place of appreciation with an open heart. We were born open hearted and vulnerable. As children, we started out by following our heart's desires. We popped that snail into our mouths because we wanted to know what that slimy little shell-encrusted critter would feel like. We then shut down our vulnerable selves in our quest for acceptance. The key is in opening to your true self, and in also appreciating the self that wants to belong to the collective. We are social and relational beings. We must advance our race from the understanding that we are all connected, but at the same time we need to honour our individuality, akin to the waves in the ocean.

There is a beautiful interpretation of a yoga sutra which talks about our true nature. We think we are separate beings, but our connected nature opens up for us when we live from our hearts.

> *"The wave forgets the truth that it is ocean,*
> *Thinking itself to be the grand shape, which it has*
> *temporarily taken.*
> *For a while, it takes on the rupa (form) of wave.*
> *Finally, it remembers its true rupa (form) of ocean.*
> *The two coexist, though one is true, and the other,*
> *though beautiful, is only relatively true.*
> *So too, we humans forget our true nature,*
> *but, through yoga, can remember."[x]*

Our true connected ocean of consciousness is within each of us as the perfection that we are. Our waves of individuality can be expressed calmly once we have cleared the rocky shores, the shadows, we formed in our early years. As children we further lost connection with our inner calm oceans as traditional education moved us from our feeling bodies into our minds. Walls were then erected around our hearts and they began to shut down as if succumbing to self-preservation from lack of use.

Those walls were further reinforced by the armour we put on as we learned to fight our opposition as lawyers. The Suit of Separation was born. All this wall-erecting and armour plating has kept us safe.

But we now need to really take a close look and ask: safe from what?

The walls we erected around our hearts as children were justified. They ensured our acceptance and survival. The Suit of Armour however, is just a relic from (dare I say it) an outdated institutionalised way of thinking. Who is really winning here? The joke is only the lawyers win, but from the statistics I've seen on depression, no, they are not winning. We must visit our shadows to deconstruct the walls we've spent our lifetime erecting around our hearts.

Once we've torn down those walls, by integrating our shadows, we will have then opened the path to our hearts. We can live from a feeling space within the present moment. We will no longer view our lives from the past moment; it will no longer haunt us. We will have rewritten the program and this program operates in the now.

Every thought you have is based on a past event. Scary really. This is why it's vital you clear up the shadows in your past so you can see a truer reality, not one tainted with the sunglasses of shame, anger, abandonment, or other special treasure.

Once you develop the skills to live more within your heart space, you will also notice things you hadn't before. There is this weird little thing called intuition. Intuition is that little ability you have, to just 'know' when something doesn't quite feel right, even if your other five senses are saying differently. It's your internal GPS that tells you to complete a U-turn when you're certain you're on the right road. It's showing you that your conscious connection is strengthening.

Another great thing which happens to you when you venture into living from your heart and not solely from your head, is that you will begin to feel (a whole new meaning of the word *feel* here) what your clients really need. They may be telling you a story, but from your intuition, you know there are probably other issues going on with them. Things you can really latch onto to help your client on a different level. You will then be the person that sees and hears beyond the surface. Now there's a skill you can show off at parties.

That's where the beauty of humanity lies. In the appreciation of each other, without judgement. Without expectation. It's a funny thing. When you learn to sit with the feeling of appreciation for others, your heart fills up and the other desires wane. The world takes on a whole new way of being to you. It looks different. Perhaps this is what it really means to become a world changer.

Calling the witness right now

Once you've truly arrived in the place where you understand emotion, with its need to be heard in you and in others, you've almost arrived. Whether you've realised it or not, I've introduced you to time travel, where you've visited your emotions in the past and projected them into the future. They are real in all aspects of time. They can affect you no matter the time zone your head is in. And the effect is felt right in this very moment.

BUT! It may or may not have occurred to you that *now* is the only time you have. Despite all those diarised court dates and deadlines staring at you. Despite your calendar full of clients that keep your mind otherwise occupied in the future moment of 'what is happening next', now is it.

You know you've arrived when you exist right here, right now.

NOW. IS. ALL. YOU. HAVE. I need you to really latch onto that principle.

Yesterday is history. Living in the past is probably not the best address on your timeline. It comes with baggage. The shadow. Your view of life based on your past experiences is a reliable indicator of your present circumstances, from your perspective only. Your future projections of what is to come are also based in memories past. Visiting a fond memory now and then, if it warms your heart with plumpness, is fine as long as you're just visiting.

In the same fashion, tomorrow never comes. To always have your mind worrying about a future event is counterproductive. First, you have no idea whether that event will occur as fortune-telling is probably not your strong point; and, second, tomorrow never comes. So, as they say in the classics 'there's no time like the present'. Yes, it's a gift. You can only shape your future from right now. This untainted, shadow-free, wonderful now.

Think about this for one second. That second is now gone. All you have is this second. Now it is gone too. I'll try not to waste your 'time' with this, but the point I'm making is all you have is this very moment. Once it's gone, it will never happen again. Read that one more time.

It. Will. Never. Happen. Again.

You might like to look at that two ways. Again, is it a good thing or a bad thing? Well, it's a good thing if you realise that every instant is fresh and unblemished, ready to start your next creation. You don't have to wait until a Monday to start something new. Now is new. Now is fresh. Your memories and future anxieties don't exist in the now at all because they dwell within the realms of another space and time.

The only way you could think that living in the now is a bad thing, is if you are not truly existing in the present space. You are imagining that something is missing; that you have missed out. It's like the parable of the person that 'would be happy when [*goal at some point in the future*] was attained'; always waiting for happiness to arrive at their front doorstep at some point in the future. These fortune-tellers have one up on me. All I know is that I've got this second.

Time is a left-brain construct. It's orderly and necessary. But only to the point that you can organise your day and be sure that your next holiday falls on the more affordable shoulder season.

Your mind plays tricks on you if you live in the future or in the past. What I'm talking about is a preoccupation with the future or the past. Not merely planning what's for tonight's dinner and freaking out because the in-laws are coming over. Nor am I referring to your grimaced reflections over which one of your precious hounds was responsible for those mysterious doggie mud prints left neatly on your white bedlinen this morning. Living in the future causes you anxiety. Living in the past causes you to feel depressed. Yes, they are feelings too, and yes, you need to feel them to appreciate that you were not living in this present moment.

Understand that you will find it a challenge to fully receive all that is offered to you in the now moment if you have tucked some of your feelings away. It means that not all of you is here now. Some of you is still living at some point in the past as that stuck child. This is why it is imperative to embrace all feelings and own them. And sweep those shadows out to dissipate into the light of day.

The principle central to you living in the present moment is that you need to *feel* what's going on, right here and right now. Neuroscientists have shown us that your heart always responds to what's going on right now. It's like an antenna. That's why you need to hear what it's saying to you. You are here to experience life. Warts and all. Yes, you can still feel angry. This is something of a problem for people. The majority of us have been taught as children that it's not okay to be angry. We should have been taught that it's okay to be angry, just don't hurt the cat, or other equally intelligent life forms whilst expressing it. You can express anger without harming anyone. Indeed, you harm yourself if you hold onto it. Like all others, anger too should be treated as energy in motion.

Whilst I have expressed my view on rules in general, this one I'm calling the 90-second rule only because in guideline naming, it rolls nicely off the tongue and is easy to remember when you are faced with a reactive moment. Much like the three-five second rule[48] one follows after one's favourite square of chocolate has landed on the floor. Instructively, Jill Bolte Taylor gives us a little run-though on what happens to us in a moment of anger:

> *"Within 90 seconds from the initial trigger, the chemical component of my anger has completely dissipated from my blood and my automatic response is over. If, however, I remain angry after those 90 seconds have passed, then it is because I have chosen to let that circuit continue to run. Moment by moment, I make the choice to either hook into my neurocircuitry or move back into the present moment, allowing that reaction to melt away as fleeting physiology."[y]*

So express that apparent negative emotion for 90 seconds, and if it's still with you for more than that timeframe, lights and buzzers should be going off because you have *chosen*, either consciously or subconsciously, to hold onto it.

All this, my dear friends, is the key to your happiness. To be happy you must put yourself in the position of receiving all that is in front of you, the whole kaboodle, right now. In appreciation for what it is. That is what being at peace is all about. Drama can be swirling about, but if you keep your focus on the now, you can really see what's happening. Your feelings will let you know if you're off course. Your feelings will guide you back to your appreciative state. Happy heart. Happy you.

Just as you have cultivated subconscious self-limiting beliefs, in his book Dr Lipton's assertion that *"Beliefs control biology!"[z]* has shown us that our positive beliefs can do magical things to our

---

48 *Allows for variations in reaction time.*

person, provided of course our subconscious mind isn't running the show. Likened to the power of a placebo, by saying beautiful affirming words to ourselves, your whole self bathes in a cleansing energy.[aa] You come out the other end all crisp and fresh, like my favourite bedsheets. Well maybe not quite crisp, but fresh is good, and it's okay if you can't see yourself as a bedsheet. You get the general idea.

The egg meditation

Appreciation and gratitude are Now's helper in this game. Being thankful for whatever it is that you can possibly thank for being in your life, is a recognition of the Now. I dare you to not feel better when you are truly staring at something in appreciation. You are then squarely in the moment. You can't be thinking about what's for lunch if you are thanking your breakfast. For instance at breakfast, you might like to give thanks to your egg. I see your quizzical expression. Let me show you how to thank a brekky egg. If you're vegan, I'm sure you can substitute tofu in there somehow. You vegans are extraordinarily clever at turning tofu into food.

I digress. Eggs. And thanking them. You can say thanks for: the fact that you can afford to buy an egg; the way you cooked it, poached to perfection; the golden colour of its yolk which complements the plate you selected to arrange it on (brekky is art if we're honest); and not least of all, the beautiful hen that laid it for us in her free-range paddock. There is a lot to be grateful for. Gratitude, when practised like this cannot do anything else but bring us good feelings in the present moment. Here we can whip up a positive thought-loop in our skilfully eggy gratitude. Sounds delicious.

I'm going all hippy on you now to let you know that you've just raised your vibe right in that moment. I'm serious. You have raised your vibe. As a result, you've followed Einstein's instructions and you've made the law of attraction be attractive in the right way. You've also reached that elusive state of inner peace.[49] Depending on your level of gratitude, you've probably even created a loving space too! Love is the highest vibe of them all. And you've done it by being present with and appreciative of your brekky egg. Virginia Warren: *President, Egg Appreciation Society.*

It might seem a little twee and silly to you; to thank your morning egg, but it really is what this life is all about. You skip over the eggy Now moments and you've missed the whole scrambled point. You've lost the plot. Especially if you broke the yolk whilst cooking it. Then is an especially great time to thank all the emotions that arise. Frustration at your somewhat less than superior culinary skills, disappointment due to your lost opportunity at cracking open that oozy yolk surprise on your plate, or even just plain amusement at your frustration. I mean, why were you getting frustrated? Who's judging you? Time to check out the shadow. It might be a little hard to swallow, but as I've said before absolutely 'everything' that is happening in your life is happening 'for' you, not 'to' you.

You've no doubt heard all the fuss about meditation and mindfulness? They are also beautiful instruments to get you to play in the Now moment. I have just taught you the 'egg meditation'; I find it starts best by focusing on your steady breaths whilst you're staring at the poaching water waiting for it to simmer. It takes a LONG time when you're staring at it.

Meditation is beautiful for this reason. Dr Joe was able to document what happens to our minds in meditation. The data shows us how being in the present moment makes the squiggly lines on the charts very squiggly. A super high vibe. He calls it bliss. Sounds good to me. All from living in the present.

---

49 *I wonder if Einstein was a closet hippy.*

I was sitting and just being[50] one day and realised that you really need to absorb the moment you're in. Soak it in, like you're receiving it as a gift. I felt the Now moment flow to me. I know that sounds a bit weird, but that's just me. Don't get me wrong. I'm constantly reigning in old leftie. I, too, get caught up in wondering what will happen next. It's a real skill to bring it back to Now. But it does get easier to do with time. Relying on expectations of what will happen next are our downfall. No-one's crystal ball is that accurate. Unplanned stuff happens, it's in your ability to look at those things from the appreciative 'is this a good thing or a bad thing?' perspective. For those of you that find it too much to let go of knowing the outcome, let's just say it will most certainly be a reliable *"we'll just have to see"*. This will break that downer thought-loop of disappointment.

Meditation is a great skill to learn for helping us find our sweet centre easily whilst we're in action. We humans are walking dichotomies. We need to remain in tune with our calm ocean within, all the while ensuring our individual wave expresses itself fully as it reaches the shore. Like a hummingbird, we need to be stillness in motion. Inaction in action. Remember, you don't have to sit in the lotus position and chant "om" to successfully meditate. An egg, your breath and simmering water are just as effective. Even just focussing on your breath will do it. There is much written on meditation and it's not all as mysterious or structured as it might seem.

Creation starts with a thought

As humans, I believe, as is the basis for this book, feelings are pivotal to our experience while doing our time here. As part of that experience, we are here to evolve, and in doing so that requires some creative skills. I think humans are doing a rather nice job of the creative component, as the exponential advances in technology

---

50 *Just being. Without reason. It's a fun thing. You should try it.*

appear testament to this.

I'm certain you have experienced the feeling of total contentment from creating something of your own. It might be anything from formulating a song parody to drafting that killer affidavit. Whatever it was, is not of importance. It could even be as inane as creating the perfect shade of 'bread beige' that you craftily assisted your toaster producing at breakfast this morning. That the creation came from your very own thoughts, which then produced within you, a feeling of complete satisfaction. This is where the present moment is essential. You cannot be creative in any other time zone. If you don't exist in this space, right now, you are preoccupied with thoughts that distort the creative process.

Being creative is like being in a meditation. It stops the incessant mind chatter. Paradoxically at the same time, it creates space for the creative thoughts to slip in. This is where inspiration is born. Thoughts are at the centre of creativity, but these thoughts tend to be more right-brained in nature. So we need to soothe our inner chatterbox.

I know when I've spent ages 'trying' to write something creative and nothing of value comes. Annoyingly, it's when I'm doing something else that the creative words flow. And I usually don't have a piece of paper. I had a barrister once mention to me that it's when he is out pruning his vines that answers to questions that were otherwise puzzling him pop right into his head.

It's also exactly the same as when you're trying really hard to remember your PIN at the checkout. Trolley full of groceries, in the holiday queue, and you have to embarrassingly leave them behind only to find that those elusive numbers pop right into your head the moment you walk out of the supermarket. Yes, I really did that. In accepting stupidity as a part of myself, I thought it was all rather funny.

Of significance is, that whilst you're engaged in something creative, time disappears. Ever noticed that? As a child, those few hours on Christmas eve took for*ever* to pass, but Christmas day was over in the snap of a cracker. You were so in the Now moment with your new toys that you didn't notice anything going on around you.

Being in the creative state or in the appreciative state, is living right IN the Now. You get out of your own way. Your single-minded focus on one task, either in appreciation or creation, puts you into a meditative state. It quiets the rest of your mind. You have given it something far more interesting to do than bother you with all your mind-bickering. This is also called creating space in your mind. You have broken free from the thought-loops. Once you can establish this kind of space, you allow your right brain to inspire you.

Even better than this, is that a positive energetic space swells around you as your electromagnetic field increases. Not only is this beneficial to your well-being, but your clients will love it too. They can feel that you are present with them. As in the tuning fork example, they can feel that you have a compassionate energy and that you are 'listening' to them. You have opened up and connected with them. This allows your client to share in that clarity and find some of their own. You didn't have to do anything 'to' them. You assisted them by just creating the compassionate energy available in the present moment for yourself. They will then take some of that beautiful energy away with them. Lawyers, offering gifts of peace. Has a nice ring to it, I think.

Your life cannot be fuller than when you give it your unconditional presence. Now is the 'in' place to be seen.

The witness – this one's reliable

Whatever we focus our attention on is what we attract. The question to be mindful of, is where are you focusing your attention? Is it on the latest drama unfolding in your life? Is it on someone else's drama? For we lawyers, it can certainly be some of the former, but it will also be a good deal of the latter. When your focus is so narrow, you become embroiled in those dramas. Literally. You are attracting some low-level vibe there, and if you tune into it, you can feel it as being close and suffocating. Heavy even. You are, at an energetic level, enmeshed.

Despite its all-consuming nature, some of us remain subconsciously comfortable and safe with this state of affairs because that energy is within us. That energy has kept us safe for a long time. As touched upon previously, this energy needs to be congratulated for its hard work during our younger lives but needs now to be recognised and released. It is no longer serving us. We do not want to remain in the heaviness of the drama. We want freedom.

If you find yourself focusing your attention narrowly, with your blinkers on, you will remain in this place. It logically follows that to move from that claustrophobic place, you need space. Let's zoom out. Let's again imagine we are in that large passenger plane coming in to land. You, you lucky thing, have a window seat.

As you sink below the clouds, you can take in the great expanse below. Meandering rivers breaking up the structured blocks of paddocks, reminiscent of a patchwork quilt. You get close to the ground, you can make out housing estates in neat little rows, some dotted with mini blue rectangles representing life-savings invested into swimming pools. Then liquorice straps for roads with little ants for cars crawling along, again in neat little organised rows. Structures. Rows. Organisation. I don't know about you, but I'm suffocating as I get closer. This was an overwhelming feeling that took me by surprise one day as my flight was about to land in Melbourne.

I looked at the roofs of all the little houses, like it was a Monopoly board. Perhaps a little on the negative side, but I contemplated the potential drama within each. I imagined all the little people waggling their little pointer fingers at each other over things from as small as the ubiquitous drama of *"What's for dinner tonight?"* all the way to, *"I want a divorce!"*. It was a bizarre sensation to zoom out from a scene and really look at it. With complete detachment. From where I was sitting, it helped me to see how insignificant our dramas are in the big scheme of things. A similar feeling to when you lie on your back and look up at the night sky.

Perspective. If you hadn't noticed already, it's a word I'm loving.

To help you engage fully with this topic, I'm going to ask you to take a moment to have a long hard look at yourself. Yes, we've been doing that throughout this book, but not in the way I'm referring to here. I want you to actually take a look at your physical self. Look at the back of your hands, turn them over and really examine your palms. Look at all the fascinating lines. Let your eyes wander. What are you seeing? You are really seeing your hands, and yes, you need a manicure. But who is seeing? Can you feel yourself looking 'out' of yourself, perhaps? Like there's someone within you doing the looking?

Try it again.

This time, notice the you that is just looking out. This experience is you being a witness to yourself. Just observing your hands. Yes, you did notice your well-overdue manicure, but to do that you had to be right in the Now moment. That is what a genius thing it is, to live from the observer perspective. It withdraws you from the outside drama to sit with a calmer non-judgmental viewpoint. Done with the intention of observing only, yes, you observe your nails need attention, but no, you didn't judge yourself for this oversight. Your observer is a valuable ally in the inner-peace game.

Being in the Now moment and viewing without judgement about all the goings-on.

Now I'll take it to the next level. Ask yourself: "*Who am I?*" Have you ever asked yourself who is actually asking that question? Who is arguing with you in your head? Where did that thought come from? All these questions, from my metaphysically-inclined way of thinking, are answered when I consider the proposition of there being a temporal self and an eternal self. I believe in this. You don't have to. That's quite ok. But it is the eternal self who is observing, the part of you that is connected at the core of your being, as in the ocean analogy. It is that objective, loving, intuitive voice that guides us, if we just care to quiet that psycho mind of ours and just take time to listen to it.

When you can objectively observe what's going on with you, in a state of appreciation for all that is, you have just opened another portal to shift your reactions. Most of us are so embroiled in our own stuff, we really fail to see what's truly going on around us. We think Jenny at the watercooler is still mad at us for what happened last Tuesday, but in fact, the reason she is not speaking to us this morning is because she's freaking out about a tax office audit. She's not talking to anyone, let alone you.

Step back, view it differently. It's not all about you from the rest of the world's point of view. People are usually too busy stuck in their own affairs to even consider what's going on in your head. As if they'd know anyway. They are equally making assumptions about your mindset. No-one knows what the hell's going on when we're all living in our heads.

From the seat of the observer, your reactions to external circumstances can be effectively moderated. That angry face staring at you could either be met with defensive anger or with the mindful understanding that the true nature of the person in front of you is not their anger, so you can then meet them with appreciation and compassion. Effectively, this is a case of developing an ability to look at what grinds your teeth; learn to see what triggers you.

Ideally, when you notice that someone triggers you, you say a mental thank you to them for bringing you this gift of awareness. If you can get your head around that, you are in the right place. Observer-mode allows you to rest in the present moment. You can observe, without judgement, how you will react. You can sit back and see your own subconscious acting out before your very eyes. It's at this point you can make the conscious choice to work on your behaviour.

In a nutshell, living from the witness perspective is another tool to assist you in reprogramming those subconscious self-limiting beliefs.

I like to look at it like I am an actor in a play, I am also the audience. As the actor, I can set the tone. The audience part of me looks on and can see what message I may, or may not as the case may be, have been able to project with my script. I choose the scripts and roles I play. Those scripts dictate my own emotional outcomes. Do I want to remain miserable? Is it a tragedy I'm conveying as my life's work? Is it a comedy? I'd prefer the latter. The audience doesn't care, it's an observer. It enjoys the entertainment either way.

CHAPTER

6

Making pain our friend

You might have decided to read this book to find out why life feels less than kissable in your day job, or in sincere search of answers to your own pain generally. Perhaps you want to feel a sense of peace whilst carrying out your life's purpose. Enough peace at your core, so that you can rise to meet your daily struggles without being thrown off balance. Ultimately that's what we all want. We know that we can't control what life throws at us, but we want to take command of our inner sanctum.

As I've alluded to, any conflict, whether bickering with your neighbour or negotiating with the chocolate you're about to eat, is an indication that something is awry within. It's a relief to appreciate there are real gifts to be found in the pain we suffer. Though to unwrap them, you will have to go through the unhappy to get to happy. We cannot extricate our intrinsic self from internal conflict until we turn toward the source, toward the painful memories that we'd rather have stay in the dark. It is then they can be validated and released so as to bring us closer to the perfection we were at birth. We can revisit what it's like to live in this world without judgement for ourselves or others, knowing that we are all, in essence, the product of some trauma or another.

This life is all about relationships.

Relationships, they're unavoidable. They are about the connection between us. Real connection. This is what we have been missing. Between us and our partners, us and our friends and family, between us and our clients. The relationship we have with ourselves, above all. Try as we might, we cannot completely separate inherent human connection. We can hold up barriers, dress ourselves in Suits of Armour, wall-up our hearts, but ultimately the consequence of this disconnection is misery. We can try and fill the void with treats, but we're beyond this ruse. We're beyond tricking ourselves. We know what is real and that is all that will satisfy us.

Without meaningful relationships we cannot survive as a species. We can choose to either point fingers in blame and reinforce the disconnection, or we can move within and connect with the part that we're playing. When we can see that our own inner battles are affecting our own serenity, it is then we truly connect, for we see that we are all in this thing together. As we decide to work on our own growth and the value we individually bring to humanity, we then serve to benefit the whole.

The law we practise is about governing those relationships external to us. Lawyers are the ones seeing the entity of relationship at its very worst. We are the ones at the end, picking up the pieces. It seems, however, the majority of us haven't been terribly helpful in advocating for the gifts. We are perpetuating the separation in the us against them mentality. I'll again ask, how can this work when as lawyers we are each advocating for our client's righteousness. Why aren't we the ones seeing this? Why aren't we the ones taking charge in turning this situation around?

If we were each able to reach our fullest expression, the relationship we have with ourselves could be nothing but harmonious. Devoid of internal conflict at best, the subject of mild fleeting banter at worst. Expression of emotion is at the core of individual human functioning and equally at the foundation of human relationships.

If you can see what you've had to endure to get to a happier place, you will without doubt be able to see your client travelling the same road. Yes, they may be dealing with different emotional baggage, but in the end it's all the same. They need to work through their own issues to become the full spectrum of emotional colour.

Complete detachment and 'not emotionally invested' are two subtly separate approaches. When we are truly acting from the place of our appreciative observer, we can help our client find their path. We can facilitate their needs and goals and at the same time know we are achieving our own. We can't do this if our left brain is in calculation mode. We need to feel into our responses, hold space for a client. Holding space is a state where your heart is open. It is connected to the plight of another but not invested in it. It's from this place that you can truly listen.

However, we are unable to hold space for another until we create the space within ourselves. With negative programming operating our lawyer-being and thought-loops entrapping and confining our energy, we have no means for clarity and spaciousness.

I have shown you that if you hold onto conflict within yourself under any circumstance, it is detrimental to your whole being. Holding onto negative emotion makes unhappy cells resulting in dis-ease. Feel it, then let it go. Do not enter into battle with yourself under any circumstances. Be conscious of the thought-loops. If you find yourself sinking, pay attention to it for a moment, then choose a lighter thought and float back up. If it happens often enough, you need to look for the cause.

Once we've been able to reprogram our subconscious to calm itself, to move to the right side of the dance of the dreaded thought-loop, we can sit in a place of peace. The peaceful inner state is who we are under the Suit of Armour. Removing the Suit of Separation connects us to our hearts, body and mind via our feelings. This place is found by using our heart-felt emotions as our navigation system. Particularly if we find the one called appreciation. It sets us down squarely in the Now moment. Tuning into this space and driving this human being using our left brain as the brilliant tool it was designed to be, the right brain as our creative connector, our appreciative heart, and our feeling body, then we have found the kissable formula.

From that platform we will then see each client that comes before us is coming bearing real gifts. Gifts for themselves. I am looking at the alchemy of conflict here. My view is that conflict can be transmuted into gold. We have all been holding onto buried treasure. Wouldn't it be a total game changer if we lawyers were the ones to hand their client the torch and say: "*Here, take a look.*

You will be in awe of what you find. You will be in awe of what your conflicted relationship has been showing you. You can now see it." Every one of us will gain insight and benefit from this liberation. The beautiful ripples created will then benefit more than those directly involved. Revolutionary!

A side, but related note, I find it fascinating that lawyers seem to be more readily challenged for seeking their fees than most other professions. We are offering a service in exchange for payment. We are, too, commercial service providers. I wondered why our profession was so singled out on this topic. It dawned on me that we appear to have garnered a reputation for charging a fee for unhappiness. Essentially, it must appear to a client that we are taking more from them than they are receiving, particularly at a time when they already feel emotionally spent. An uneven bargain, perhaps? People move toward what makes them feel happy. My imagination tells me that perhaps they don't want to spend their hard-earned dollars on something that's unpleasant. I know I don't. No offence to my dentist, who's a lovely person besides.

We can change this, too. Let's give our clients value for each legal dollar they spend. Collaborative lawyers are doing this already. We can even take this further by showing a client the alchemy of conflict, their hidden treasures, in exchange for the money they spend with you, they will feel better for having met you. You are giving them something real to take away from the legal, and dare I say it, life conundrum they find themselves within.

They will benefit from your presence in their life for the rest of their days.

That's real value all 'round. Positively affecting the lives of community can only benefit the reputation of the legal profession. Your client feels better. You feel better. Armed with this knowledge, you can now take Adam Liepzig's life-purpose quiz and show how your service in the practise of law changed someone's perspective on life. For the better. You can look forward to saying you're one of the happy 20% at your next reunion. What a thought!

This vision I have, albeit a grand one, can begin with you.

I dare to dream.

Brief to counsel

Most of us know that we need to exercise, eat more healthily, drink enough water and get plenty of rest. That's the physical body taken care of. But the mental body, our thoughts and feelings, equally need our attention.

We've used our IQ to understand the importance of EQ, so here's the triage if you need the ER to locate your peaceful, innate state of being.

Own your shadows

It would seem logical to start work on unlocking that which has restrained us from reaching our peaceful state. The Suit of Armour, now fondly recognised as the Suit of Separation, the ego, is what we first might have thought to be our nemesis. It has clouded our minds with shadows and prevented us from not only fully opening to who we really are at our core but has been the predominantly inhibiting factor in our ability to connect with our hearts and in turn, the rest of humanity. However, in making it our ally, and thanking it for its protection, we have opened space for it to return as a valued and integral part of us. Which, once welcomed home, enables us to view the world with a softer more peaceful gaze.

Once all aspects of ourselves are home, we can then take care of our other needs, such as honing our skills of appreciation to get us into the Now moment, where all good things happen. It is for this reason I am, at the outset, giving the shadow special celebrity treatment.

I believe this psychology has been overlooked in the majority of 'self-help' regimes out there for lawyers. Primarily, because it requires us to move toward our feelings of discomfort. It's also time to move away from solely external gratification, from anesthetising our traumas with medications or burying them in addictive behaviour. We need to fully immerse ourselves in our unpleasant feelings if we are to allow them the recognition they're screaming for, and the space to integrate. Whatever we resist persists.

Recall that our limiting subconscious beliefs are formed due to the suppression or disowning of a feeling or emotion in the early stages of our lives. This forms a shadow aspect of our self. As our hearts have been protected, they will also remain closed. Walled-up. Shadows, as we know, cannot exist in the light. To release our inner conflicts, the suppressed feelings now need to be expressed. The tricky part in dealing with the shadow is that you don't know what you don't know. Hence its shadowy descriptor.

> We must move our emotions from
> suppression to expression.

Below are some steps to bring your shadows into awareness. This step-by-step guide is by no means exhaustive, but in my experience is most suitable for those subconscious beliefs that are readily surfacing and wanting your imminent attention:

1. Recognise that a shadow is within your midst. You will notice this has occurred primarily in your reactions with

other people. These are specifically reactions that occur regularly, which are either: disproportionate to the action; or, are retained by you and extend way past the 90-second rule.

2. Feel those reactions. Feel them deeply. Acknowledge their existence and validate them as truly belonging to you. Do not supress them. That said, be sure not to further inflict the reaction on others around you. The principle of non-harm applies here. Note: you will continue to harm yourself, via the retention of internal conflict, if you keep the feeling suppressed.

3. Thank the feeling and the situation for arising and showing you its existence. This thanking step is critical for bringing all awareness of the feeling to the present and eliminating your personal conflict with the feeling. Sit with the feeling of gratitude that you have created. If the suppressed feeling is brought readily to your awareness in this step, this may be sufficient to offer you some immediate relief.

4. If you cannot yet feel relief, given the shadow formed in the past, you will then need to revisit any memories you associate with those feelings – the earliest memories that bubble to the surface. Do not force a memory. Your subconscious will allow whatever it is you need to reflect upon in that moment to arise for your benefit. If it is at all practicable, carry out this step the moment the triggered feeling arises.

5. Your feelings within the memory need validation. You need to be able to visit that memory and say, it was right and acceptable to feel sad, silly, angry etc. This validation sets your emotion free to flow on through you. It is no longer trapped in the unacceptable zone.

6. Acknowledge that you are the adult now, and that you

appreciate that supressing the emotion kept you safe while you were young, but you and your power of choice are now here to keep you safe.

7. Sit with your eyes closed, focusing on your breathing to establish heart coherence and envision yourself in future scenario expressing that emotion as a true and valid part of you in an appropriate way. Feel into what that now looks like for you. It is important to feel this as something happening right now. Feel it in your heart.

Bear in mind that during this work, you are healing yourself. You are the only one that can do this. Your broken arm healed itself from that skiing debacle. No-one, but no-one can heal you. People can assist you toward healing if you can't face the suppressed emotions on your own. Others can provide support but only you do the actual healing. This is central to your progression. Rely on someone else to help you feel better and you are, again, giving your power away. You were the one that disassociated from certain emotions, and you alone will be the one to retrieve them.

Yes, you can reach out to others for guidance and inspiration. Of course, people can be there to facilitate your progression. Just do not follow others like they have the answers external to you. The solutions all lie within you. The doctor will reset your broken arm, but it is your own physiology that gets to work on the healing. Your mind and body want to remain in homeostasis. That notion is at the core of your operating system. You are meant to be well. Simple.

This is not a definitive work on integration. There are many resources available on working with the human shadow; however, fundamental to all the work is that you must bring your self-limiting beliefs into awareness. This takes differing timeframes, subject to one's own resistance. Sometimes, you will notice that as you integrate, as those wayward aspects of your being come home, you start seeing the world differently.

For instance, you may have resolved your feelings of being victimised and so you will no longer attract power trippers into your life. Your life will start looking more authentic. This can, at first, be a little unsettling as these shifts take place. You are shifting a status quo, removing the walls around your heart that have been in place for longer than they should. Naturally this will evidence itself in some discomfort. But if you are open to this understanding, you realise you are setting yourself up for a more creative, connected and therefore fulfilling life experience.

This work clears a way from head to heart. You've built that armour of protection around your heart, you've kept it safe. Now it's time to liberate it.

Rebuild the connection.

The one JOB we all must do.

To start rebuilding our connection to all that we are, breathing must take pole position on your To Do list. Breathing, I think you will agree is not only good for our health, but is a trait humans tend to have in common. It's in *how* we breathe where we differ.

Imagine, if you will, that for the 'perfect' human lifespan, we come complete with a finite amount of breaths. If that were the case, I would like to make those breaths deep, long and of a high quality. But how can we manage that task consistently when we find ourselves in stressful situations where we become so overwhelmed that we're very nearly at the point of hyperventilating?

In the hyperventilating picture, which many of you will be rather familiar with, you will experience many short, sharp and difficult breaths. With that in mind, now think of your life as a journey of breaths. I don't know about you but short, sharp and difficult doesn't translate into the type of life I'd want to live. In every great journey, it's reassuring to remember that it all begins with the first step. Breaking hard tasks down for you, I can now reveal that you only have one real JOB to focus upon:

`Just. One. Breath.`

Just taking that first one deep breath when in the midst of a meltdown immediately does a few beneficial things to your body:

1. Your parasympathetic nervous system becomes a team player and like a good parachute, it floats you back down to earth as it calms you. Let me tell you, this is one system I want acting on my behalf at all times. Your heart rate slows. Your digestion improves. Detox is going on. It's amazing.

2. Your focus on that one breath transports you directly into the Now moment.

3. And if that's not enough, I have one additional immediate benefit that might appeal to your vanity. Your posture improves. You'll look more impressive than you already are.

All in all, the step of taking Just One Breath works as a supercharger for your entire system. The added bonus is you carry it with you as an as an on-the-go remedy whenever and where ever you need it. The more often you can remind yourself that all you need to do is take that one long deep breath, the more readily you are able to take those long deep breaths on autopilot. If there has been no other reason to put the proverbial oxygen mask on yourself before others, then this is it.

You may now agree that all this breathing is good for you, but you may also now want to know how it's done... *correctly*.

This may sound a little weird, but not many people really know how to execute a worthwhile breath. You see a baby breathe and their little bellies rise and fall. As we get older, most of us lose that skill and only take short shallow breaths into our chests. Effectively we are only using a portion of our lung capacity even when we are in a relaxed state. Remember what I said about quality of breath relating to quality of life. Short and shallow, or long and substantial? Your call.

Here's an exercise to help you understand how to create your best breaths:

1. Lie comfortably on your back and place a book or other object on your stomach that won't easily roll off.

2. Start by breathing as you would normally, ensuring that you breathe in through your nose and then out through your nose.

3. Then take a deep breath in through your nose counting to three so that you make the book rise up. Then breath out again through your nose for the count of three. You are now breathing into your belly. This is fun! You can do that a few times, watching your book sailing the sea of your belly, or you can graduate to the next step.

4. Now you're going to breathe into your belly for the count of three, then continue to breathe in for a *further* count of three into your ribcage so that it expands. Then slowly let the air out of your ribcage for a count of three, then all the way out of your belly, so it drains completely out of air, for a further count of three.

5. Last round, if you're ready. Breathe into your belly for a count of three, continue into your ribcage for a further count of three. Then, this part takes some practise. If you can,

continue to breath in for a *further* count of three so that you imagine your breath filling up your shoulders. It is at this point you should feel a wonderful expansion in your upper body.

6. Then slowly reverse this process. Deflating your shoulders, your ribcage, your belly each for a count of three. Now you will feel a beautiful release.

Congratulations, you have just practiced the three-part yogic breath.[51]

When you are able to do this smoothly, you will have the JOB system at your ready in any immediately stressful situation. You can leave it there if you wish. That will be enough to give you instantaneous results. For me, I like to take it up another level. As I'm engaging in my on-the-go yogic breath, I like to imagine that I am breathing in warm, cleansing sunlight[52]. As the breath fills me up to the tops of my shoulders I picture the sunlight cleansing all negative energy as it radiates out of each pore of my body. There I stand energised and bathed in my inner sunlit glow, whilst everyone around me is in meltdown. Try it. It's a breath in the right direction.

Connecting to the now, connects to the heart

I've just shown you how to place yourself squarely into the Now moment via your breathing. Breathing properly is a precursor to experiencing all that Now has to offer you. Meaningful breaths also open the pathway to your heart. This is great news because via that simple JOB you are starting to make some important connections. Yes, JOB comes complete with an internal social aspect too – deepening the neurological connection to your heart.

---

51 *I'll secretly make yogis out of you yet!*
52 *Please feel free to substitute any other kind of light that tickles you, moonlight, candlelight, purple light, it's all up to you really.*

To live from our heart means we must exist in the present moment. This takes practise.

Similar to the function of the neurons in your brain, the neurons in your heart will also require some firing up to firm up those connections. After you have checked in with any subconscious beliefs you may still be nurturing, you may have now put yourself in a position to embrace living in the Now moment. This is the most powerful space you can be at any time. It is also the only place that you can reside in peace. It is from here that you can be that picture of stillness in motion. It's the only place your heart knows. To live in its presence you must live in the same time zone, and that, of course, is right Now.

Now removes you from any clouds of the past. It's so yesterday. So unfashionable. You are out of the mind chatter. You are out of your own way.

I have set out below some useful tips for you to reflect upon to help you find the Now. If, at times, you are not feeling your highest of vibes, you can run down the list to see if something resonates with you.

To shift toward a stronger heart connection takes gentle practise. We've had our heads rule us for most of our lives, I promise you, your ego doesn't want to let go of control that easily. This is why you meander into this shift gently and with patience. Let go of outcomes. There is no goal to achieve. No winning line to cross. You are simply seeking to breathe fresher air. It's a continual process. Your challenges and rewards keep coming. You are exercising your power of making choices to view the challenges as also being the rewards.

Not one method should be preferred over another, and please do not ritualise anything to the point you become trapped by it. You do things because you want to, not because you have to. *Feel* into your choices. It's then you retain your personal power.

1. I know I'm repeating myself, but I cannot emphasise this enough. This list topper serves as a prompt for you to remember your JOB. Just One Breath. Breathe in the NOW. Breathe in deeply as an on-the-go pep up. Again, you can do it surreptitiously. Everyone breathes, you're just doing it mindfully to kick your parasympathetic nervous system into gear. Remember that your breath and your heart are intimately connected. Your heart only operates from what is going on right now. Your unconditional presence is the key to connection with yourself and others, and Now is the only place that can occur.

2. Appreciate. Appreciate. Appreciate. Appreciate everything. It's happening for you, not to you. Express gratitude, wherever you can.

3. Move from your intellectual mind into your feeling body. You are all there, use it or lose it. Recognise you've found your heart, now Feel. Feel. Feel. Feel everything. The cat, that fluffy new 'blankie', your heart break at a sad movie, how the jam donut burnt the roof of your mouth. I don't care what it is, FEEL it. Exercise those feelings and they will become so familiar that you will be able to tune into the feelings of others in a heartbeat. Melt that Suit of Armour.

4. Caveat to point 3. In the event of a negative feeling, check in to see whether it got you all entangled in a thought-loop. If so, give the emotion its 90 seconds of fame and motion it onward. If you can't move past it, a shadow may need your present attention.

5. Savour the food you eat. Again, connecting to the physical. If you are going to ritualise anything, make a ritual out of your eating habits. You have to eat. You might as well make it

ceremonious. This practise has the added bonus of removing any conflict you have with eating. You are choosing to engage in it, and you are sensualising it. Sight. Smell. Touch. Taste. You can listen to it too if you so desire. Yes, chocolate speaks volumes.

6. If you're in a meeting with intense individuals, observe the people you are with from a standpoint of curiosity. Ask yourself a few questions about them. What are they feeling and why? How did they get to this place? How are their challenges serving them? How is their attitude helping you? What benefits can you obtain from this situation for your own growth?

7. Further to point 6, use stealth. Be stillness in motion. When in the middle of a crisis, shift your perspective into the seat of the Big O. The observer. No-one will know you're doing it, and they will think you are cooler than a cucumber. This gets you right out of the fire until you've taken that deep breath ready to step back in with a calmer centre. You become aware of yours and all other players' actions from a non-judgemental point of view. Here you are safely in the Now moment. The power of choice is Now yours to exercise calmly. The calmer energy you bring forth will positively affect those around you. You're the actor, rewrite the script. Added bonus: your empowerment to choose how you react to a given situation is another brilliant means of reprogramming any self-limiting beliefs you may be still be holding onto.

8. If you're feeling emotionally tangled, find somewhere to go outdoors, if you can. Take your shoes off. Stand on the grass, sand, soil, whatever you can get your feet on and feel your energy connecting with Mother Earth. If you are not in a position to do the former, then use wherever you

are and 'imagine' yourself making that connection. Gently close your eyes, or if you prefer, keep them open with a soft gaze. Take some deep relaxing breaths. On your outward breath feel your spent energy flowing into the Earth and being transmuted. Mentally thank Mother Earth for taking your scribbly vibe and on your next breath in, feel the fresh grounding energy flow up through your body. Repeat until you feel a sense of calm overcome you. This is a lovely meditation, and no-one ever has to know you're doing it. You are transported right to the Now moment, where clarity is found.

9. Choose a better thought and 'feel' it. You not only break a thought-loop, creating heart coherence, but you also command your mind into a preferred future right from this very point in time. Feel the tension flow away from your body in this state. Feel your energy field expand and become lighter.

10. Meditate. This can mean just mentally focusing on the movement of your breath. All meditation means is stilling your mind to connect with your innate state of being, using a point of focus, like doing the dishes or washing the car. It's not complicated. If you are still uncertain, there is plenty of valuable reading material available and some designed specifically for lawyers.[ab]

11. If you remember that the world is your mirror, see those that trigger you as an aspect of yourself. Even more so, given the notion that we are all one, everyone is just an aspect of you. It's just a beautiful way to view others. You realise that everyone has their own journey, their own hurdles to overcome. I sometimes like to people-watch, just to see if I can guess what it is that they might be here on this planet to do for us all. A fun pastime.

12. Thank 'everything' that happens to you. Firstly, from the perspective you are currently in, you are unaware of whether it's a good thing or a bad thing. Nevertheless, it's a gift whichever way you look at the situation. Second, gratitude brings you back to the present moment and raises your vibe.

13. Spend time nurturing your body. It is not only your vehicle taking you places; your body is an integral part of the whole of you. It feels your feelings and communicates those feelings to your heart and mind. Keep it well and in coherence by doing anything that helps it to feel delicious to you in the Now moment.

Way to start the day

On a final self-care note. I'm not one for rituals, if someone tells me I 'have' to routinely do a certain thing for my betterment, I feel like I've given my freedom away. When studying various philosophies on how to enhance my life experiences, I found that many told me I had to be a certain way. Sit with your legs crossed, hold your breath, breathe into your belly, nose pointing north, surrounded by tulips, under a quarter moon and all will be well. Not one of them was wrong, and some of these ideas seemed to be working for some good folks for a very long time. Yet, I felt not all of them could be the only ones who were right.

It was indeed all too much dogma for me and my cat to grapple. I decided therefore that it was much easier for me to partake in those practises that 'felt' good to me. If it means to me that I want to be sitting still one day, then I'll do that. If it means doing a few breathing exercises another, or yoga poses another, then that's what I do. The point is, I avoid conflict with myself. I don't want to have to get up every morning and feel guilty if I do not go for that

5 km run for instance.[53] I elect not to feel as if I'm under some sort of self-imposed pressure to do anything.

That said, it is wonderful to get yourself going for the day with the best vibe you can. If there is anything I can 'recommend', it is checking in with your thoughts the minute you regain consciousness. Your thoughts first thing in the morning are a real indicator of how you're travelling. If you've tuned into anything that worries you, you are not in the present moment. In fact you are existing somewhere else in time.

Don't judge yourself for those thoughts, just notice them from your observer perspective. Like, a surprised, *"Oh! That's what we think we were going to think about today?"* Then just take a second or two to pause, breathe really deeply and find something to be grateful for. It could be simply that you have some warm slippers to put on, or that the there is a roof over your head. Then drink some fresh water. You need to plump up your cells so that they transmit the thoughts of gratitude your having to get the good thought-loops in motion for the day.

After that, the day is all yours for your own expression. Try to make your day a day of choices rather than obligations. If you can, try to devote some time to pleasure each of the parts that are you. Your mind, your body and your heart. Then, in the words of Thaddeus Golas, *"Whatever you are doing, love yourself for doing it"*. This may seem an odd statement, but it means two things: 1) You are choosing not to live in a state of internal conflict; and 2) As you fall into closer alignment with your truest unshadowed self, you will instinctively make the best choices for your greatest internal fulfilment.

Finally, if you want to max out your day, remember to soak in the Now of every moment. It's all you have.

---

53 *To be clear, this is an example for all you peeps that love running. I choose not to run. It is a powerful choice I made some time ago that running and I remain respectfully distant from one another.*

The evidence – almost happily ever after

For me, seeing my life from a new perspective has worked out rather well so far. I had not imagined myself as a creative person in the least, due to being all maths and science in school. And up until year 12, I considered myself to be a fine English student also, that was until I dismally failed an English essay. That was the moment my identity as a 'straight A' student was, from where I sat, cruelly snatched away from me. Those 'A's were who I was.

That one failed piece of writing pretty much was the beginning of the downward spiral for me. My self-worth was based upon my perceived intelligence. Those numbers on that sheet of paper told me, in red ink, that I was stupid. Not only was I stupid, I was also, according to the remarks written on that paper *"self-conscious and contrived"*.

At 16 years old, with my many other shadows, I had absolutely no idea what that meant, and indeed I could not comprehend it, which served only to add to my stupidity. Doubly stupid and now it seemed, to my teen mind, utterly worthless. My grades were my only saviour, and this was my 'strike three, you're out' moment. It was clear I'd now proven to myself that I was totally unlovable. Enter cheese-toasty addiction and weight gain, reinforcing said unlovability. This seemingly minor addiction morphing later into more grow-up ones like cigarettes, wine, shoe shopping and last but not least, chocolate.

Working with my shadows, I became aware of that aspect of self-consciousness, found my creative voice and started writing. My humour may not be to everyone's taste, but it's mine and I own it. The quotation by Alan Wilson Watts at the start of this book says it all. I needed to say this, no matter the consequences. Tip toeing around what I believe to be true has now become the antithesis of my purpose.

If someone judges me harshly, I can now appreciate that this is their shadow talking. If I've unintentionally bothered someone with my words, I know that I may just be shifting them from their seat of comfort. It just might be some notion within them is tapping on their consciousness asking to be heard, hopefully opening some valuable dialogue. I'm no longer that sixteen year old seeking approval.

Like most of us, I have been through the proverbial wringer in this lifetime. But I've been the lucky one. Nothing has happened to me by accident. It's all happened for me, not to me. It's all perfect. I found the alchemy in this experience called life and I look forward to the next thrilling instalment.

It is with my deepest appreciation for you, that I hope you can do the same.

ENDNOTES

a https://map.gsfc.nasa.gov/media/080998/index.html. *Retrieved 7 October 2018*

b *Jill Bolte Tayor Ted Talk Ted2008 My Stroke of Insight https://www.ted.com/talks/jill_bolte_taylor_s_powerful_stroke_of_insight*

c *How to know your life purpose in 5 minutes | Adam Leipzig | TEDxMalibu. https://www.youtube.com/watch?v=vVsXO9brK7M*

d *Goleman, Daniel. Emotional Intelligence. Bloomsbury Publishing. Kindle Edition*

e *Goleman, Daniel. Emotional Intelligence (p. 18). Bloomsbury Publishing. Kindle Edition*

f *Dunne, Claire. Carl Jung: Wounded Healer of the Soul: An Illustrated Biography (Kindle Locations 2130-2131). Watkins Media Ltd. Kindle Edition*

g *Eliade, Mircea. Shamanism Archaic Techniques of Ecstasy (p. 27) Princeton University Press, 1964*

h *Ingerman, Sandra. Soul Retrieval: Mending the Fragmented Self. HarperCollins. Kindle Edition*

i *Eliade, Mircea. Shamanism Archaic Techniques of Ecstasy (p. 217) Princeton University Press, 1964*

j *Simeona, Morrnah, Self-Identity through Ho ' oponopono, Basic 1, (p. 36) Pacifica Seminars (1990)*

k *Lipton, Bruce H.. The Biology of Belief 10th Anniversary Edition: Unleashing the Power of Consciousness, Matter & Miracles (p. 122). Hay House, Inc.. Kindle Edition*

l *See, for example, Rose, Yvette, Metaphysical Anatomy. ; Lipton, Bruce H.. The Biology of Belief 10th Anniversary Edition: Unleashing the Power of Consciousness, Matter & Miracles (p. 129). Hay House, Inc.. Kindle Edition*

m *Watts, Alan. Psychotherapy East & West (p. 164). New World Library. Kindle Edition*

n *Supernatural pp29-30*

o *Lipton, Bruce H.. The Biology of Belief 10th Anniversary Edition: Unleashing the Power of Consciousness, Matter & Miracles (p. 80). Hay House, Inc.. Kindle Edition*

p *Lipton, Bruce H.. The Biology of Belief 10th Anniversary Edition: Unleashing the Power of Consciousness, Matter & Miracles (p. 139). Hay House, Inc.. Kindle Edition*

q *Supernatural pp33-34*

r *Supernatural pp35-35*

s *Supernatural p 27*

t *Blake, William in letter to Trusler, dated 23 August 1799*

u https://www.heartmath.com/science/ *for full article*

v *https://www.heartmath.com/science/*

w *https://www.heartmath.com/science/*

x   Swamiji's Interpretation of Patanjalis' Yoga Sutra 1.3 http://www.swamij.com/yoga-sutras-10104.htm

y   Taylor, Jill Bolte. My Stroke of Insight (p. 146). Hodder & Stoughton. Kindle Edition

z   Lipton, Bruce H.. The Biology of Belief 10th Anniversary Edition: Unleashing the Power of Consciousness, Matter & Miracles (p. 129). Hay House, Inc.. Kindle Edition

aa Lipton, Bruce H.. The Biology of Belief 10th Anniversary Edition: Unleashing the Power of Consciousness, Matter & Miracles (p. 129). Hay House, Inc.. Kindle Edition (p. 131)

ab See, for example, Cho, Jeena and Gifford, Karen. The Anxious Lawyer: An 8-Week Guide to a Joyful and Satisfying Law Practice Through Mindfulness and Meditation (2016)

ACKNOWLEDGEMENTS

Putting together this book was a scary endeavour, especially for a person who was pigeon-holed by her Year 12 English teacher as being *"self-conscious and contrived"*. That deflating description cloaked me so tightly in a lifetime of doubt, ensuring that my writing of anything remotely resembling creative remained a writer's job, not mine.

In the world of no accidents, it took a visit to a psychic to get me writing. She told me I needed to write. Apparently, it was my life's work. I laughed at her. Loudly. She even went so far as to buy me a pretty pink journal to be sure I would follow through on her advice. That she had so much faith in her own craft, and in me, I thank her from the depths of my heart. Thank you Emma Skeggs for believing in me.

To my beloved husband, Shane. You've patiently listened to my ramblings over the past couple of years as the ideas for this book were taking shape.

Ariel and Grace Warren, the most delightful newlyweds I've met. Your young marriage and sights set on an adventurous future together does nothing but warm me through. You both are the epitome of free spirits, accepting the ebbs and flows of what life deals you with open hearts. I love you both dearly. Please never change.

Going the indie publishing route for this book was like doing a nudie run with words. Both daunting and exhilarating. So my deepest gratitude extends to all those involved in getting my message out to the world. To Julie Postance for her sound advice and guidance in connecting me with the myriad of people necessary to bring life to a book, without her I would have not had a clue. To the patient Amanda Spedding for even agreeing to tackle my dubious writing style with her editor's prowess. To Sophie White for her talents in bringing these pages to life.

To the legal system. Thank you for getting me so annoyed with you for moulding your lawyers into icicles that needed thawing. And for my resultant need to eke you out of your institutionalised ways by breathing some fresh air into your cold halls. Whilst I am rather good at breathing, I wish myself luck on the latter point.

And a sincere thank you to all the other kind beings that I've encountered in life's classroom. I appreciate your ready agreement to undertake a role in this play called my life. Without each and every one of you, there would be no story to tell.

ABOUT THE AUTHOR

Have you noticed that some people tend to measure their self-worth by the certificates they hold? That idea bugs me a little, so I suspect I have already told you something about myself. I am not something that can be measured. But I guess for the purpose of letting you know where I'm currently at in this game called Life, I have to do the same. I understand that if I'm going to have a chance at being heard, I need to have a recognised knowledge-base upon which to draw, as is expected of authors in these types of ventures. If you were to take a look at the current certificates that proclaim some of my identity, you could say, among other things, I'm a legal practitioner and yoga teacher.

As a result of this book, it would appear that I am now also a writer, which is something I'm extraordinarily proud of. This writing business was a hurdle I needed to overcome to find the 'self' in my own self-consciousness. I measure my self-worth in how well I can sit in peace with my good self as opposed to what others label my self-worth as being. My self is worth a good deal more to me now than it was when I was younger. The value has come in the recognition that the sometimes-painful twists and turns of my life has helped me relate to other people.

I do not hail from a background of privilege, that is, if you define privilege in a monetary sense. And the lessons I endured in life's classroom including sexual abuse and family breakdown, took me much self-loathing and many addictions to work through. Privilege to me, I was to later discover means having lived through those experiences and understanding the real meaning behind them.

My journey into law afterwards was full of high heels and ideals, but reality bit hard. As most lawyers, who think like me will tell you, the novelty wears off after a while.

A wayward encounter with my leopard-print stilettos then found me accidentally in a yoga studio. It was there I finally understood what all of life's rotten stuff was about. A portal opened to a whole new way of existence. I could now see the world in such a way that I became frustrated that others couldn't readily see it. I had to learn to tone that down. I understand that there are those that are ready and waiting to see a new perspective, and there are those that are not. It's all perfectly as it should be.

Invariably, I thought I should put all this energy I'd garnered to good use. I started getting ideas. My day job and personal pursuits started merging. Could I emulsify law and yoga? Could such ideologically-opposing practices co-exist? I started looking at wellness resources for lawyers to discover there's wasn't an overwhelming amount out there. It's not a popular subject. Vulnerability is not the industry buzzword.

I've more recently completed training in shadow work and collaborative law and maintain an interest in many spiritual philosophies. I'm now a vegetarian that doesn't drink alcohol, smoke and avoids cane sugar. Vices that once gave me fulfilment have fallen away as my alignment with me became stronger. There may still be a little shoe shopping and on that note, I embrace my humanness.

Emotional empowerment for lawyers is now my game plan: "*If you don't find your emotions, they'll find you and it won't be pretty*". Oh, my qualifications for this game are sound. I've lived through them all.

Life responds to emotions, and so I verily believe that lawyers' ability to tap into this inner resource will produce a follow-on shift in the practise of law.

SERVICES

As a conflict alchemist, Virginia provides guidance to separating couples, and to others embroiled in conflict, on ways to view that conflict from a positive perspective. She enjoys helping people recognise and unwrap the gifts to be found in the otherwise traumatic circumstances arising in their lives.

Via her Lawyers' Life Mastery program, she empowers lawyers emotionally, offering them tools to work with this alternative approach in improving the way they practise law, benefitting not only their clients, but also themselves.

Virginia's alternative perspective teaches you that the way to live this life with real meaning is by embracing life's tricker moments as exciting opportunities for growth, rather than as scary ones to avoid.

By arrangement, Virginia is also available for speaking engagements, seminars and personal life-enrichment training.

e: letschat@virginia-warren.com

w: www.virginia-warren.com

Lightning Source UK Ltd.
Milton Keynes UK
UKHW020320200123
415634UK00001B/14